FLAVORS FROM THE FARM

FLAVORS FROM THE FARM

Vegetable-Forward Food to Share

EMMA HEARST

weldon**owen**

This book is dedicated to the small farms and artisans out in the world doing beautiful, difficult, and meaningful work.

CONTENTS

SOUP & SALAD TIME

FRIENDS & FAMILY

SWEETS & TREATS

OTHER USEFUL TIDBITS

"To be a good cook, you have to have a love of the good, a love of hard work, and a love of creating."

—JULIA CHILD

ABOUT THIS BOOK

WARNING: This cookbook is neither vegetarian nor vegan. It is instead a book where vegetables and fruit are held in the highest regard, occasionally dancing with meat or fish. This is indulgent vegetable-forward cooking. In these pages, produce takes center stage on the plate rather than being an afterthought to a roast. You will not learn how to truss a chicken or how to smoke a brisket, though those are very useful things to know. You will not find recipes requiring avant-garde tools and a degree in culinary or baking arts, and you will most certainly not find anything strict or rigid. We are not out to emulate Escoffier.

Forts Ferry Farm is a collective of chefs, agricultural technicians, hospitality professionals, artists, and innovators who believe in the profound power of food. We grow vegetables, fruits, flowers, and herbs that all shine in their own unique way. Our seeds are steeped in history, each one having a story, no matter how commonplace they might be. Most often, the more ordinary types, such as carrots, onions, radishes, and garlic, have the greatest difference in flavor when compared with their mass-market counterparts, and they happen to make some of the most delicious dishes too! We pick and choose each variety with the intention of diversity and the most flavorful outcome, growing them all in the most natural of ways, always chemical-free.

This book is filled with unfussy recipes meant to inspire a great meal at home. It places importance on finding the best ingredients one can possibly source to create homemade meals using classical methods in casual ways. These are recipes that hold a steady charm while being communicated in an honest tone. Everything here has been written with the assumption that you, the reader, are smart, curious, and able to think for yourself when in the kitchen.

When placed in the starring role, rather than the shadows, produce must be carefully selected and prepared in a highly diligent way. Eaten alone, rather than as an accompaniment, vegetables and fruits begin to take on a different light. Their beauty and flavor stand out as boldly as their imperfections. The mind-mouth connection becomes acute to the differences between freshly harvested produce and the stuff that has been kickin' around in a climate-controlled warehouse for months. The quality of the produce you use is vital to the quality of your cooking.

In order to cook simple, straightforward dishes, every ingredient needs to be the best of its kind, from the salt near your stove to the herbs for your garnish. When the ingredient list is tiny, everything must be mighty, and your kitchen should be stocked to be the most functional and useful expression of yourself.

We will occasionally express strong opinions on certain topics that really matter, all of which hopefully will inspire you to incorporate farmers' market hauls into delicious daily routines. And butter . . . there will be butter.

After reading this book, if you hold a deeper respect for produce, then we've succeeded in our task. We hope you understand a little more about the hard work it takes to make food grow and that you will go on to seek out the farmers, foragers, and artisans who are making a positive impact on our world with their practices. We hope you'll gain the confidence to try new things, observe and learn from your mistakes, and use these pages as both inspiration and reference—but never gospel.

Most of all, we hope you get outside in the fresh air, plant a seed, and watch it grow. Lure your family and friends into the garden and kitchen to make great food—and have fun with it! Remember that small farming is the past, but it's also the way to the future.

The Conduct of the Kitchen

Good cooking comes from a handful of great ingredients, the most indispensable one being flexibility. Precision, unless carried out to the most finite degree, can often be more misleading than vagueness. When ingredients are kept loose and narrative, it gets the home cook to move, innovate, and improvise, to head off to the store and the pantry to discover new inspiration. It encourages creativity to come about based on what the cook comes across. If you dare to tinker, this book will not let you down.

Most of these recipes do not apply the pressures of last-minute timing and preparation. Many are quick to produce or can be completed ahead of time, allowing the cook to enjoy the best part of the process, the entertaining. Substitutions and adaptations are encouraged so cooks can create versions authentic to themselves, which in itself is a true luxury.

Select a handful of recipes that align with the seasons, occasions, or emotions to create a fabulous spread to share with friends and family, all in the name of fun!

Having the *right* ingredients and materials at hand encourages the best kind of cooking: impromptu.

Nothing fancy is needed to have a smoothly functioning kitchen. The more you embrace procuring the items necessary to have a well-stocked pantry, the more you can work with simplicity and ease—and the more money you'll have in your bank account too! A thoughtfully outfitted pantry provides the foundation necessary for improvised cooking.

Think of the refrigerator, freezer, and even the herb garden as different wings of your "pantry," working hand in hand with the dry goods portion. They all need to be well stocked in order for the kitchen to work as a cohesively brilliant unit.

You don't need an abundance of condiments or obscure ingredients—though they *are* fun to buy and try! You do, however, need the *right* ones to provide the foundational infrastructure that supports the versatility of what you may need or want to make at any given moment.

Tools

When it comes to tools and utensils, your hands are always the most important consideration. Collect a few select blades and some well-crafted pots and pans that you love to hold. Invest in resilient motor-based tools and a small number of no-frills hand tools. That is all you need! What you save on passing up superfluous tools gives you much more room to splurge on tasty ingredients. This, combined with a basic level in technical understanding and a well-stocked pantry, will set you free!

Salts

Diamond Crystal kosher salt is the salt used throughout this book. It has a rather mild flavor that makes it much more forgiving when dialing in the right salinity. It is also additive-free, unlike the tainted canisters of table salt decorated with little umbrellas. To finish dishes, we rely on beautiful, delicate flaky sea salt, such as Maldon from England's Essex County, which has a glassy texture, crystalline structure, and high crunch.

Lemon

Second only to salt in seasoning, freshly squeezed lemon juice (and other citrus too) can turn the most tasteless of dishes into a radiant delight. Beyond its use in a vinaigrette, a squeeze of lemon enhances flavor when it plays with salt, it cuts fat from the most unctuous meat, and it will even clean your copper pot after you cook in it! Its more operative part, the zest, contains beautiful aromatic oils that, when added to nearly everything from cocktails to braises, make them better.

Oils

Olive oil from Greece, Spain, Italy, California, and beyond all have varying degrees of fruitiness, spiciness, bitterness, and best uses. It's wise to stock a variety that ranges from buttery to peppery and then always have a neutral one on hand as well. Grapeseed oil is a good choice for a neutral oil with a high smoke point that can be used for making aioli and searing meat.

Vinegar

Stocking a full spectrum of vinegars will take you far in the kitchen. It is just as important to have basic white wine or rice vinegar as it is to have a bottle of elegant aged sherry vinegar or syrupy balsamic. Selecting the correct vinegar for a dish and adding it in the proper amount can make all the difference to the success of the finished dish.

Stock

One of the all-time-great kitchen essentials never to be without, stock is easily made from the remains of any chicken dinner or a plethora of vegetable trimmings, simmered with a handful of herbs and aromatics. A homemade chicken or vegetable stock will surely be better than any store-bought. For chicken stock, a whole bird will certainly do, but chicken wings and feet will make for the richest stock due to their cartilage. Beef broth is not something we often make at home, so I always keep a few containers in the freezer.

Sweeteners

Dark maple syrup, local honey, and agave nectar are wonderful to have on hand for both sweet and savory applications.

Tomato Products

A couple of tubes of tomato paste and a few cans of San Marzano peeled whole tomatoes are always wise to have in stock for whipping into an effortless and satisfying pasta sauce (page 224).

Dried Beans

Forgo the canned bean. The flavor of canned beans can never match the flavor of cooked dried beans. The latter require not much more effort than the foresight to begin soaking them in cold water the night before you plan to cook them. They can be transformed into an elegant dish on the fly, and are particularly useful when you cannot stand over the stove, as they can pretty much cook on their own, with just a check-in now and again.

Grains and Pastas

Having several whole grains and pasta shapes to choose from can make for many exciting meals. Farro or bulgur can be mixed into a roasted vegetable salad, a bag of freshly milled polenta or grits makes for a creamy side or a cake, and a few types of rice, both short and long grain, are ideal for stuffing peppers or cabbage or for a simple pilaf.

Nuts and Seeds

Virtually indispensable in any well-stocked pantry, kitchen, or even purse! Toasted in the oven, nuts and seeds immediately evoke a cozy atmosphere. They have a way about them that breathes life and depth into a dish that might otherwise be mundane.

Extracts and Pastes

This is not the place to go cheap. Sourcing only pure products—never ones with a label listing chemicals and additives—will always give you the best result. To make your own vanilla extract, see page 193.

Spices

The spice cabinet should be stocked with the right ones but not with an overabundance. You want to routinely go through this section of your kitchen to make sure you don't hold onto those that have lost their pizzazz. I always buy whole seeds rather than ground, as the flavor quality is profoundly different. Spices like cumin, nutmeg, coriander, and cinnamon are much better grated or ground in small quantities as needed. Once ground, they rapidly lose their intensity and develop a soapy flavor.

Peppercorns

Remember that although black peppercorns often sit with salt, they should never be treated the same way. Salt enhances the flavor of whatever it touches, whereas black pepper imparts pepper flavor. Therefore, we always treat pepper as a spice, using it often but only when we want the flavor of pepper. In this book, when we call for black pepper, we are always referring to freshly cracked from a grinder. Pre-ground pepper has an entirely different flavor and should never be used. Pink peppercorns have a soft texture and can be smashed in the palm, while white pepper is used so infrequently that we just buzz up a little in a spice grinder when needed.

Pickled and Brined Foods

Always keep a stock of pickled and brined goods that can be brought out for entertaining on a whim. This includes different mixes of olives, spicy pickled vegetables for charcuterie boards, and beautiful briny capers or green peppercorns for sauces, dressings, and dips.

Tinned Fish

Simple, flavorful, convenient, and nutritious—you can't go wrong if you have an assortment of these pocket-size friends scattered around the kitchen ready to use. Since they contain only one or two ingredients, quality will always stand out, and bad products don't have a curtain to hide behind. You want to source quality here because you are in fact dealing with fish . . . in a can! When you taste a really good one, you'll know.

Flour

Many cooks don't realize that flour actually goes rancid quite quickly. A small stock of a nice all-purpose and a couple of more nutrient-dense whole-grain flours, like buckwheat or rye, is really all you need.

How to Blanch a Vegetable

A perfectly blanched vegetable is a skill that few know how to execute well. It's one of our favorite ways to prepare our glorious produce for all kinds of uses. Here's how we like to do it.

Get a large pot of water—larger than you think you'll need—and bring it to a boil. Add a fistful or two of kosher salt, stir it around, and give the water a taste. It should be as salty as the sea. Remember, this is your chance to season the interior of whatever it is you're blanching. (The same goes for pasta water.)

While the water is heating, get an ice bath ready— equal parts water and ice cubes in a big bowl—and place it near the stove along with a slotted spoon or pair of tongs.

Once the water is at a rolling boil, begin adding the prepped vegetables, working in batches. The key is to not overload the pot. Make sure the vegetables have room to float freely in the water. *Pay attention.* This shit moves *quickly*.

Let the vegetables cook for about 20 seconds and then give a piece a try to check its tenderness. If it's "crunchy tender," pull all the pieces out and submerge them in the ice bath. As they cool, they will continue to cook a little more in their residual heat. Once they are cool, drain them and give them a pat dry.

Depending on how you plan to use what you're blanching, you may want to alter the cook time. For example, if you will be giving the vegetable a second cook on the grill for some char or in a cast-iron skillet for a crispy exterior, you should absolutely blanch it for less time so it doesn't turn to mush in the end. If you are serving simply blanched vegetables on a crudité platter, you will want to really nail the "crunchy tender" timing so they feel pleasant in the mouth.

How to Build a Menu

Designing a first-class meal at home requires two important ingredients: a hefty dash of common sense and a basic understanding of how to handle the ingredients you are working with. Ingredients must be carefully bought, traditionally cooked, and presented in a lively manner that takes the diner on a satisfying adventure. The bottom line is that a well-crafted menu is best when all its courses are consistent in quality, very fresh, and, just very, very good.

Each recipe selected to compose a meal should play its part in making the meal a treat while still being extraordinarily simple to prepare. When planning, seek and pay attention to contrast, which is the most important thing in any composed dish or menu. Contrast should be reflected not only in color and other visual cues but also in texture and in the manner in which the ingredients are cooked. Too much of the same makes for a slog of a journey rather than one paved with exciting twists and turns. This is particularly important to consider when you are working with a short menu, as contrast becomes much more apparent. For menus of six courses or more, you can get away with remixes of certain flavors, textures, and temperatures if you pace them correctly. There should be an engaging blend of textures with varying levels of richness so as to not leave the diner overwhelmed or, even worse, underwhelmed.

Think about timing when plotting out a meal at home, and envision how it will all come together in the end. It is quite unwise to have more than one course that requires last-minute preparation, unless you're assisted by a small team or have an affinity for masochism. You will inevitably become flustered and pissed off, and will lose the game of mastering of the meal. An intricate cold first course can be

assembled with calm ease and concentration if you have chosen a braise for the main dish, which can be left unattended in the oven to simmer away to blissful perfection.

Last but not least, consider making something you've never made before. Remove yourself from the stereotypical box you've constructed by busting out something new, but give it a trial run before the big day to know that you can execute it successfully. Oftentimes, ingredients and dishes are ruined by timid cooking. Be bold, move with confidence, and take it to the edge! You might be surprised by what you find.

FARM BEVVIES

One might not always be at a party, but one can always strive for a better time.

SUNGOLD GIMLET

■ **SERVES 1**

These plump orange cherry tomatoes might as well be sugar cubes. Sungolds have a supersweet, fruity, and almost tropical flavor with a thin skin. They are prolific producers and are always the first tomatoes to ripen in the summer and the last ones to be removed from our greenhouse in the fall. Because of their outstanding flavor and disease-resistant qualities, they are popular among many farmers, so odds are you will be able to source them from your local farmers' market—if you aren't already growing them yourself. We typically look for more obscure varieties for planting, but Sungolds are the exception and *always* make top priority on our yearly crop list.

4–6 Sungold cherry tomatoes (some for the cocktail, some for the garnish)

2 oz gin, plus a splash for good luck (we like Martin Miller's and think it tastes like diamonds)

¾ oz fresh lime or lemon juice

Up to ¼ oz simple syrup (page 27), optional

Fresh buxom basil leaf, for garnish

HOT TIP For a larger batch, zip up all the ingredients in a blender and strain. Then shake with ice and strain into a coupe.

Muddle as many Sungolds as you like in the bottom of a shaker. Pour in the gin and lime juice. If your tomatoes are very sweet, skip the simple syrup; if not, adjust the amount depending on their sweetness. Fill with ice, cover, and shake vigorously until well chilled and the ice has broken down a bit.

Strain into a chic vintage coupe and garnish with a pick threaded with as many Sungolds as you like and a billowy basil leaf.

THE DRUNKEN BEE

■ SERVES 1

Not all honey tastes the same! Honey harvested at different times of the year will have different strengths and flavor nuances—lighter in the spring, darker in the fall. It's wise to choose the type of honey according to the type of cocktail you'll be making with it. Milder honeys, which are usually lighter in color, lend themselves to more acidic, bright cocktails, while richer, deeper-hued honey is best suited for drinks made with darker spirits. Before making a cocktail, give your honey a taste and adjust the ingredient proportions accordingly.

2 oz whiskey

1 oz fresh lemon juice

1 oz honey simple syrup

Honeycomb cube and bee pollen, for garnish

In a shaker, combine the whiskey, lemon juice, and honey syrup. Fill with ice, cover, and shake vigorously until well chilled and the ice has broken down a bit. Strain into a chilled cocktail glass or coupe. Garnish with a drippy cube of honeycomb speared onto a skewer and a sprinkle of bee pollen.

Fun Variation: If I have a vanilla bean lying around, I like to scrape a few of its seeds into this cocktail or into the simple syrup for added depth.

SIMPLE SYRUP

In a small saucepan, combine equal parts filtered water and sugar over medium heat. Bring to a simmer, stirring until the sugar dissolves. Then remove from the heat, let cool, transfer to a jar, cap tightly, and store in the refrigerator. It will keep for a few weeks.

HONEY SIMPLE SYRUP

For some cocktails, you may want a honey flavor, which can be achieved by making a honey syrup. Make it just like simple syrup but with honey in place of the sugar. Stronger-flavored honeys work well with a 1:1 ratio of water to honey, while lighter honeys work better with a 1:2 ratio or even less. Store as for simple syrup.

A BLOODY FORTS FERRY MARY

■ SERVES 8–10

Complicating something does not necessarily yield a better result. We have found this to be true with the Bloody Mary. Our recipe calls for Zing Zang Bloody Mary mix, a superb base. Some might ask, why wouldn't you make your own concentrate from the tomatoes you grow? Well, we have tried, and the result didn't turn out to be better. So let's keep it simple with the mix.

Any Bloody Mary worth doing is worth overdoing, so if there is ever a time to load up a glass with excessive garnitures, this is it! Go all out here! Go absolutely nuts! Get weird. If you are seriously hung over, which most of us are when seen consuming a Bloody Mary, then just seek the path of least resistance in your garniture search. Keep it fresh and simple with a cleansing wedge of lemon and a crunchy rib of celery. One Bloody Mary is about all my acid reflux can handle, so it's my only opportunity to nail the finish. I like mine super-duper spicy and fully loaded with crunchy goodness for dipping.

FOR THE MIX

4 cups Zing Zang Bloody Mary mix

¼ cup fresh lemon juice

¼ cup Worcestershire sauce

¼–½ cup prepared horseradish

1–10 shakes hot sauce, such as Crystal or Tabasco

Pinch of celery salt

Freshly ground black pepper

Small piece fresh horseradish root, peeled

—

Vodka (2–3 oz per cocktail)

Garnishes

To make the mix, in a large pitcher or other vessel, combine the Zing Zang, lemon juice, Worcestershire sauce, prepared horseradish (amount depends on how cool you are), hot sauce (it's your call on heat level), celery salt, and several aggressive grinds of pepper. Using a Microplane or other fine-rasp grater, shower in a little fresh horseradish. Stir well, taste, and adjust the seasoning to suit your palate. If not using immediately, cover and refrigerate until needed.

To make each cocktail, pack a tall glass full with ice. Pour about 4 oz mix and the vodka over the top and stir for a hot minute until chilled, then garnish away! Just make sure to serve with a stick of sorts, such as celery, for stirring the drink to get all the good bits that settle on the bottom.

GARNISHES

- Pickled vegetables of any type except beets
- Carrots, radishes, or Hakurei turnips
- Blanched sugar snap peas
- Little Gem leaves
- Celery rib with frilly leaves—always
- Cucumber spears
- Cured meats, such as dry salami, mortadella, prosciutto cotto, country ham, jerky, or crispy bacon
- Green chile rings, such as Anaheim or poblano
- Crispy pepperoni
- Olives of all types
- Marinated cheese chunks, such as feta
- Anchovy fillets and other tinned fish
- Pickled peppers
- Flowering herbs like basil, cilantro, papalo, or pipicha
- Citrus wedges
- Cherry tomatoes
- Fried shallots
- Raw oysters or other chilled seafood

LAVENDER & HONEY GIN FIZZ

- **SERVES 1**

Lavender is something we planted on the farm our first year, only to forget about it for quite a long time. Years later, the big patch we had planted had grown into a substantial crop. Wanting to make room for more herbs to come, we decided to harvest it all and try to sell it at our local farmers' market. We tied it up in swanky little bouquets and it was sold out within a matter of hours, making for the most profitable market we attended that year. It beat all of our farmers' market revenues of the past. Who knew we had sat on this purple-hued gold for so many years!

Here, lavender bitters flavor a fizz, an old-school cocktail that combines a spirit, citrus juice, a sweetener, club soda, and sometimes an egg white. Two things to know about lavender and its primary types: English lavender has a sweet taste, making it well suited for culinary purposes. It has grayish stems and can often be substituted for herbs like rosemary. French and Spanish lavender are much more potent and typically not the best for cooking. These two types are better placed in a sachet to tuck into a sock drawer or scent a powder room. All lavender is quite slow to mature in East Coast climates, but if you get a successful variety, it is definitely worth the wait.

2 oz gin or tequila

1 oz fresh lemon or lime juice

¾ oz runny spring honey

1 large egg white

Dash of lavender bitters

Splash of club soda (about 1 oz)

Lavender sprig, for garnish

In a shaker, combine the gin, lemon juice, honey, egg white, and bitters, cover, and shake vigorously for at least 1 minute. This is called a dry shake and will help the cocktail develop froth (from the egg white) and have a better mouthfeel without ice diluting the mixture. Add a handful of ice and shake vigorously once again until well chilled.

Strain into a chilled highball glass, top with club soda, and garnish with the lavender sprig.

OUR MARGARITA

- **SERVES 1**

The margarita is one of life's most refreshing beverages. Although I have nothing against premade mixes, this is no place for one. Nothing, I repeat *nothing*, can take the place of freshly squeezed citrus. I like to use lemon juice, rather than lime, for the base of the drink and then place a meaty wedge of lime on the rim for the garnish, but feel free to switch the citrus as you like. Muddling a few hot chile slices, herb leaves, or pieces of fruit can also make for a really spectacular and satisfying variation.

Fine kosher or sea salt and citrus wedge, for rimming the glass

2 oz tequila or mezcal, or 1 oz of each!

1 oz fresh lemon or lime juice

¼ oz Grand Marnier

1–2 barspoons runny honey or agave nectar

Lime wedge or orange slice, for garnish

Spread a small amount of salt on a flat saucer. Rub the citrus wedge along half of the rim of a rocks glass, then roll the dampened edge of the glass in the salt to coat (coating only half allows sipping flexibility). Fill the glass with ice.

In a shaker, combine the tequila, lemon juice, Grand Marnier, and honey. Fill with ice, cover, and shake vigorously until well chilled and the ice has broken down a bit. Strain into the prepared rocks glass and garnish with a lime wedge or sprig of herbs.

LET'S TALK BOOZE

Every house needs a respectable inventory of spirits, wines, and beers for drinking and cooking along with all the bits—tools, glassware—that makes handling them a pleasure. Here are some tips to make the pour or the simmer go smoothly.

Serving and Drinking Wine

Get a great wine opener, specifically this one: Pulltap's Classic 500. It's the only thing you'll ever need. Throw out all those cheap wine accessories given to you by your in-laws and family members on holidays past, and never look back.

Purchase a Champagne bottle stopper because you want to keep those bubbles flowing! TableCraft model 398 is the best. I keep one around every corner.

The body of the wine counts for more than the color. You can serve a light red with fish or chicken because it is light in body. The *body* of a wine refers to the weight of its mouthfeel and taste. For example, a bold white Burgundy or oaky Chardonnay would overpower delicate raw dishes. A good rule to follow is to pair delicate dishes with higher-acid, lighter-body wines and more robust dishes with bolder, big-boy wines that will stand up to them.

When in doubt, always go the sparkling route! Sparkling wine or Champagne is a friend to nearly every dish no matter how lowbrow, highbrow, delicate, or heavy it is. It is a particularly refreshing contrast to anything fried.

Give your light reds like Gamay or Beaujolais a slight chill, and watch your guests' eyes light up on a sunny fall day.

Good Champagne should never commingle with orange juice, and good orange juice should never be tainted by Champagne.

Making Cocktails

When it comes to cocktails, simple is best and quality is key. Invest in solid barware and glasses. You'll need two sturdy, no-fuss all-stainless shakers, a mixing glass, a barspoon, a strainer, a jigger that feels good in the hand, a set of great all-purpose coupes, a set of great highball glasses, and a set of great rocks glasses.

Don't subscribe to recipes that use seventeen ingredients. They will just give you a headache to make as much as a headache after. Skip the gimmicks. Keep your beverage very alcohol-forward. That's my kind of drink.

Don't ever serve stale ice. The only thing worse is serving someone a dead cat. Ice is extremely important in cocktail making. When stirring or shaking the cocktail, a bit of the ice melts and integrates into the drink, so the spirits and the ice must be perfectly palatable in every way.

Never pour anything into a hot glass unless you want to piss someone off or you're serving a hot drink. With drinks you are serving "up," that is, without ice, do your guests a favor and chill the glasses in the freezer or with some ice before filling.

Never use citrus from concentrate. Use fresh or none at all.

Cooking with Alcohol

Some say the better the wine, the better the dish, and many times that is true if the dish is wine-forward. But I say cheap wine is better than no wine at all for cooking—and in desperate drinking times too! If you are making a beef bourguignon or red wine–braised turnips, you will certainly want to use something finer than box wine. However, if you are giving a quick deglaze to a pan or need just a bit of acid, nearly any wine will do. For this reason, I like to keep a "nice" box of wine in my refrigerator at all times.

Having a stock of not only wines but also beers, spirits, and liqueurs for cooking will eliminate the need for many random pantry ingredients. They don't need to be super extravagant in price or size. Here are the ones I always like to have on hand in my household: basic red and white wines; sherry, Madeira, and Marsala; port and Sauternes; a few sturdy beers and stouts; and a selection of spirits and liqueurs, such as whiskey, rum, Pernod, brandy, Grand Marnier, and Kahlúa.

When cooking with wine or spirits, use more than you think is needed because much of their taste evaporates in the cooking. But when finishing a soup with a bit of wine or tossing fruit in some liqueur, always err on the side of a light hand. And, for God's sake, never mix your boozes. You will inevitably end up with a soapy, perfumed, muddy mess that tastes reminiscent of bathroom cleaner.

PAPALO

PAPALO MOJITO

- **SERVES 1**

Papalo is a bluish-green leafy herb that is native to Latin America and is widely cultivated throughout Mexico. Its taste and smell are unique, refreshing, and hard to mistake. If cilantro, arugula, and mint had a really clean baby, it would be named Papalo! This herb is difficult to find in our area, which is why we love to grow it. It makes for a lush and fragrant patio plant, but if you choose to plant from seed, be sure to get more seeds than you think you might need as it tends to have a low germination rate. The soft, wide, gently scalloped leaves are beautiful to use in salsa, cold noodle dishes, soups, and floral arrangements, but be sure to use the leaves before they get too big. Overly mature papalo plants can become woody and unpalatable. If you hate cilantro, then odds are you won't like papalo, so use mint or basil in its place.

3–6 fresh papalo leaves, depending on maturity

1 teaspoon superfine sugar, or ¾ oz simple syrup (page 27)

2 oz mezcal or rum, plus a splash for good luck

Juice of 1 plump lime

2 dashes of grapefruit bitters

2 oz or so club soda

Orange, lime, or grapefruit slice, for garnish

In a highball or collins glass, muddle the papalo leaves and sugar to release the flavor of the leaves. Add the mezcal, lime juice, and bitters and give a few good swirls with a barspoon. Pack the glass to the rim with ice and top off with the club soda. Garnish with a citrus slice.

MY MARTINI

■ SERVES 1

Most purists will scoff at the mention of vodka in a martini, but that's fine! Scoff away. Gin doesn't always get along with everyone, and I prefer the nothingness flavor of vodka. I also prefer my martini shaken, not stirred, to the point that diamond-like vodka crystals form on top when it's poured into my chilled glass. My martini wants to be adorned with many garnishes, far more than just one skimpy olive. While this might not be the way purists serve this classic drink, it's damn delicious and it's my way.

Splash of dry vermouth, for rinse

2½ oz vodka or gin

Drop of olive brine

Lemon twist, for garnish

2 or 3 olives, preferably Castelvetrano with pits or stuffed when in the mood, for garnish

1 or 2 cocktail onions, 1 pickled chile, or 1 pickled green bean, for garnish

Pour the splash of vermouth into a chilled—I repeat, *chilled*—martini or Nick and Nora glass, swirl it around to coat the sides, and pitch the rest.

In a mixing glass or shaker (no judgment here, though, as you already know, I like mine shaken), combine the vodka and olive brine, fill the glass or shaker with ice, and either stir or cover and shake vigorously until *very, very, very cold*. Strain into the prepared glass. Load it up with all the garnishes on skewers while breathing in pure anarchy.

AN ANYTIME SPRITZ

■ SERVES 1

Spritz time is a ritual for many, particularly on the Amalfi Coast of Italy and throughout Spain. At its center is a curiously uncomplicated beverage that demands the drinker sit down for a break, reflect, and breathe the day in. This particular spritz is a simple vermouth version. Aromatic wine vermouth has become popular in the boutique spirits world. You can now find truly fine small-batch vermouths with a depth of flavor that will blow your mind, especially if you have tasted only the generic ones.

This cocktail is perfect for people who have a lower tolerance for alcohol—hence, I don't drink it much. But when I do, I find it pairs wonderfully with food and is prime for sipping at any time of day. You'll have to drink a few to figure out your favorite ratio, of course, but when in doubt, 50:50 always delivers a respectable cocktail.

---

3 oz vermouth of choice

3 oz soda water

Very fun garnishes of choice

Fill a wineglass with ice, preferably crushed or tiny cubes, and pour the vermouth and soda water into the glass. Give it a swizzle with a cute stick, garnish, and serve with gusto!

HOT TIPS FOR GARNISHES

For white vermouth: Garnish with cucumber ribbons, torn celery leaves, and even a couple of buttery Castelvetrano olives. I love a citrus peel strip of lemon, bergamot, or Buddha's hand as well.

For red vermouth: Garnish with a slice of punchy citrus. I also love to throw in a sprig of a woody herb, such as rosemary, thyme, or marjoram, that has been kissed by a flame to bring its oils to life.

BANGIN' BAR NUTS

When I was in my late teens, I worked at the Union Square Cafe in New York City. One of the first things I was allowed to make were their complimentary bar nuts. They were so good—sweet, salty, spicy, and crunchy bits of fatty and unctuous chew—truly the perfect package for keeping guests imbibing at the bar. This recipe is an homage featuring our farm's dynamic hot peppers, which we dry every year for our bangin' chile powder.

    4 cups unsalted raw nuts, such as peeled hazelnuts, peanuts, cashews, pecans, walnuts, or almonds
    1 cup raw pumpkin or sunflower seeds (optional)
    1 cup dried large coconut flakes
    3 tablespoons butter
    2 tablespoons firmly packed brown sugar
    1–2 teaspoons cayenne pepper or hot smoked paprika
    Leaves from 2-4 sprigs fresh rosemary or sage, roughly chopped
    Kosher salt
    A twinkle of Maldon salt

Preheat the oven to 350°F. Spread the nuts and seeds (if using) on a sheet pan. Toast, stirring once or twice, until golden and aromatic, 10–15 minutes. Toss the coconut flakes on top for the last minute.

While the nuts are toasting, in a heatproof bowl, combine the butter, sugar, cayenne, rosemary, and salt. When the nuts come out of the oven, immediately pour them into the bowl holding the seasonings and mix thoroughly. Once they have cooled slightly, give them a taste. They should have an equal balance of sweet, salty, and spicy and be just bold enough to make you want more. Adjust with a bit more cayenne, sugar, and salt if needed.

The nuts are excellent served warm but are equally good at room temperature. They will keep in an airtight container at room temperature or in the refrigerator for up to 2 weeks.

Note: If you are in a household with nut allergies, we love this just as much with pretzels or with a nut-free homemade snack mix. Use the same seasoning mixture, but disregard toasting the nuts and skip right to tossing everything together, then bake until golden, 5–10 minutes.

COCKTAIL SOUR CHERRIES

Our son, Georgie, loves to go out for "cocktails." He tends to order a Shirley Temple (or a Roy Rogers) with a pint of cherries on the side. The kid eagerly devours the neon-toned cocktail fruits, while we wince at the amount of red dye no. 40 he is consuming. Since we have cocktails a lot at home, we knew it was time to make our own dye-free cherries that would be much better for his health.

Come late spring, we always make sure to source the best we can find from surrounding farms in the Hudson Valley since our cherry trees aren't quite mature enough to fruit. These are far superior to even the nicest jarred cherries available and take mocktails, cocktails, and ice cream sundaes to the next level.

Be sure to start with clean cherries.

    1 lb sour cherries, such as morello
    1½ cups Luxardo maraschino liqueur
    ⅓ cup tart cherry juice
    Heaping ¼ cup sugar or runny honey, to taste
    Dash of vanilla bean paste or pure vanilla extract
    Pinch of kosher salt

Stem and pit the cherries and pat dry. Put them in a heatproof bowl.

In a saucepan, combine the liqueur, cherry juice, sugar, vanilla bean paste, and salt and bring to a simmer over medium heat, stirring until the sugar dissolves. Remove from the heat and pour over the cherries. Let sit until cooled to room temperature.

Transfer the cherries and their liquid to an airtight container and refrigerate. They will keep for up to about 1 month.

GINGER & TURMERIC HOT TODDY

- SERVES 2

This simple creation is not only comforting on the coldest of days and nights at home but also has medicinal benefits to cure all that ails you even on the finest day of health! Made with or without alcohol, it should leave you feeling invigorated and might even lessen inflammation, too!

2 cups filtered water

2-inch piece fresh ginger, thinly sliced, or a few fresh ginger leaves

2-inch piece fresh turmeric, thinly sliced

Pinch of whole cloves, plus more for garnish

Runny honey, for sweetening

1 lemon, halved, plus 2 lemon slices for garnish

Bourbon or rum (about 2 oz per cocktail)

In a small saucepan, combine the water, ginger, turmeric, and cloves, and bring to a simmer over medium-low heat for about 20 minutes. Remove from the heat. If continuing right away, strain the water and discard the spices. For a supercharged version, let cool, then transfer to an airtight container, refrigerate overnight, and strain the next day before continuing.

Return the infused water to the saucepan and bring to a gentle boil. Divide the water between 2 heatproof glass or ceramic mugs. Add a drizzle of honey to each mug, stir to dissolve, and then squeeze in a bit of lemon juice. Add the bourbon, and stir again. Garnish each mug with a lemon slice and a few extra cloves.

FALL SQUASH & BERGAMOT BUTTERED RUM

- ■ SERVES 2

Cue autumnal tones, plaid shirts, and crunchy dying leaves! According to Wikipedia, buttered rum was thought to be a nutritious beverage that strengthened the body during the colder months. This is great news, and it's honestly how I feel about adding butter to anything. Remember, butter makes it better!

8 oz water

2 teaspoons loose Earl Grey tea, or 2 Earl Grey tea bags

4 oz aged dark rum

¼ oz orgeat syrup (optional)

2 drops pure vanilla extract or vanilla bean paste

2 tablespoons Fall Squash Compound Butter (page 229)

3–6 whole cloves

3–6 whole allspice berries

Dark maple syrup, for drizzling

2 bergamot twists, or 2 drops bergamot essential oil and 2 lemon twists, for garnish

In a saucepan, boil the water. Add the tea and brew very strong. Remove from the heat and stir in the rum, orgeat syrup (if using), and vanilla.

Divide the hot tea mixture between 2 teacups. Finish each cup with half each of the butter, cloves, and allspice, and a small drizzle of maple syrup. Garnish the rim of each cup with a bergamot twist or add a drop of bergamot essential oil to each cup and garnish with a lemon twist.

FARM LEMONADE

■ SERVES 10–12

We use a tremendous amount of fresh citrus in our recipes, and we regard its importance as nearly equal to salt. For the citrus that have been used only for their zest, we always make sure to juice in routine batches to avoid waste. We incorporate the juice into various sweets and other recipes throughout the year, but during the peak of summer, our favorite use is to turn it into big batches of herby lemonade for our team to enjoy. We love to serve it up with a splash of seltzer, and often add a quality vodka, gin, or tequila to take the edge off long, busy days.

8 cups filtered water

2 cups fresh lemon juice, strained

$2/3$–$3/4$ cup agave nectar

Peel from 1 orange, in strips

A thoughtful mix of fresh herbs and their blossoms, such as lemon verbena, anise hyssop, Thai basil, mint, lavender, rosemary, and/or thyme

HOT TIP We love all herbs with this, but our most favorite is a mix of lemon verbena and fluffy anise hyssop blossoms.

In a large pitcher or other vessel, combine the water, lemon juice, $2/3$ cup of the agave nectar, and the orange peel. Stir and mix well. Taste and add more agave nectar if needed. Cover and chill in the refrigerator for at least 20 minutes.

When ready to serve, pack glasses with crushed ice and pour the lemonade over the ice. Garnish with herbs and herb blossoms and enjoy.

FRESH RASPBERRY & APRICOT RUM SLUSHIE

■ SERVES 6–8

A year or so after acquiring the farm, we attempted to drill a couple of wells for water on our new property. It turned out to be more difficult than we thought. Little did we know the farm was sitting on a thick blanket of shale. The wells we drilled would either produce very little water or collapse in on themselves within a matter of weeks. After several attempts and very little luck, we decided to enlist the help of a local dowser to locate a few promising spots for potential wells. He showed up to the farm with his divining rods along with a gift of raspberry plant clippings from his property. We planted them in a patch that week and have been propagating them ever since into a much larger plot. They fruit a few times every year from summer through fall and produce some of the finest raspberries we've ever tasted. The dowser's water-source recommendations did not prove to be much help, and we still don't have well water, but the raspberries live on!

10–12 sweet apricots, plus fresh sliced apricot for garnish

2 cups frozen raspberries

12 oz white rum

8 oz fresh lemon juice

4 oz honey simple syrup (page 27) or runny honey

1–2 oz orgeat syrup

Pinch of vanilla powder

Pinch of kosher salt

Torn fresh basil leaves, for garnish

Cut the apricots in half and remove the pits. Lay the apricots in a single layer in a large ziplock bag or on a sheet pan and place in the freezer until frozen, about 4 hours.

In a blender, combine the frozen apricots, raspberries, rum, lemon juice, honey syrup, orgeat syrup, vanilla powder, salt, and a hefty handful of ice. Blend until smooth, thick, and cohesive.

Pour into tall chilled, glasses and garnish with fresh apricot slices, fresh raspberries, and a few basil leaves.

PARSNIP PAINKILLER

■ SERVES 1

I liken the parsnip to the carrot's somewhat peculiar sister. It is the perfect shade of dirty white and has an unmistakable nutty, grassy flavor. Parsnips must be harvested with care, as their leaves contain a skin-irritating compound that can cause a painful "parsnip rash," which feels like an extreme sunburn. On a more upbeat note, we love the flavor of parsnips so much that one day we decided to juice them and make a cocktail. Their flavor ended up pairing nicely with sweet pineapple, inspiring a riff on the famous tiki drink the painkiller. It's a unique spin on the classic that is sure to numb any pain you might have from the harvest. If parsnips aren't your thing, carrot juice is a perfectly fine substitute.

3 oz parsnip juice

3 oz pineapple or fresh orange juice

2 oz dark rum

2 oz Coco López cream of coconut

Pinch of kosher salt

Freshly grated nutmeg, for garnish

Pineapple wedge, for garnish

Dark maple syrup, for garnish

Salted macadamia nuts, for snacking

In a shaker, combine the parsnip juice, pineapple juice, rum, cream of coconut, and salt. Fill with ice, cover, and shake vigorously until well chilled and the ice has broken down a bit. Fill the most fun glass you can find with crushed ice and strain the mixture over the ice.

Garnish with a few rasps of whole nutmeg, a pineapple wedge, and a teeny drizzle of maple syrup. Slip a big-ass straw into the glass and enjoy with a side of macadamia nuts in a dark candlelit room, letting all pain slip away.

MELON-COLADA

■ SERVES 8–10

We dabble in melons from time to time. Some turn out great, others not so much. They not only take up a tremendous amount of space in our plot but also attract many pests due to their high sugar content. The fruits that make it out of the field unscathed usually end up getting processed into purees for palletas, gazpacho, or sorbet. We generally have had the best luck with the pocket-size varieties, like the Charentais melon, a luscious orange petite cantaloupe of French descent, or the Early Silver Line, a crunchy pear-like Korean variety. Although you can never quite tell what will be inside all of those shifty-eyed melons until you crack them open, here are a couple of tips to help identify a good one: First, give them a good squeeze. Your fingers should not find soft spots on the rind. Then give their butts a sniff! They should smell sweet and fragrant, with no hint of compost. Cantaloupe varieties work best in this recipe, as they tend to add a creamier consistency than the more water-heavy types, like honeydew or watermelon.

About 4 lb cantaloupe-style melon, peeled, seeded, and cut into 1–2-inch cubes, plus cold melon wedges for garnish

12 oz Coco López cream of coconut

10 oz white rum

4 oz coconut milk

4 oz fresh lime juice, plus lime wedges for garnish

Kosher salt

Dark rum, for float (about ½ oz per cocktail)

Maldon salt and chile powder, for garnish

16–20 Cocktail Sour Cherries (page 43), for garnish (optional)

Lay the melon pieces in a single layer in a large ziplock bag or on a sheet pan and place in the freezer until frozen, about 2 hours.

Once the melon pieces are frozen, it's time to get cocktail crazy! Divvy up the ingredients—melon, cream of coconut, white rum, coconut milk, and lime juice—into two batches for the best result. Put one batch into a blender, add a tiny pinch of kosher salt, and blast the blender on high while in a swimsuit with a pool of water in sight. Once you have a frozen, creamy, and smooth texture, pour it into tall chilled glasses. Hold a barspoon upside down over the top of each drink and slowly pour dark rum over the spoon, layering it on top. Serve the first round to the nearest lucky few, then repeat.

To make a larger batch in advance, you can blend the two batches and put them in the freezer. Just before serving, return each batch to the blender and blend again, then pour into glasses, top with the dark rum float, and serve to your eagerly awaiting guests.

I love to garnish this cocktail with an icy-cold melon wedge sprinkled with a little Maldon salt and a hit of our heirloom chile powder for a kick. A lime wedge on the side is a must, and if you're feeling extra fancy, finish with a couple of homemade cocktail cherries.

FRENCH TOAST EGGNOG

■ SERVES 8–12

French toast has been a morning passion of mine ever since I was a little girl, when I would make it for weekend breakfasts with my dad. The batter was always more creamy than eggy and had too much vanilla, plenty of freshly grated nutmeg, and a hit of orange juice or zest. Eggnog is very similar to the base of French toast, only it is heated in a pot. The flavors for this decadent drink are bold, and I always use the amazing eggs from our farm hens. It is a wonderful holiday sipper and also fantastic to use as the batter for French toast cooked up in brown butter in a cast-iron pan.

½ gallon (64 oz) whole milk

2 cups sugar

2 cinnamon sticks,
plus 1 stick for garnish

24 large egg yolks (the best
quality you can find)

1 vanilla bean, split lengthwise
and seeds scraped from pod

Grated zest of 1 orange

Pinch of kosher salt

2 cups cold heavy cream
(the thickest, richest cream
you can find)

12–20 oz booze of choice

2 whole nutmegs, for garnish

In a heavy saucepan, combine the milk, sugar, and cinnamon sticks over medium heat and bring to a simmer, stirring until the sugar dissolves. Remove from the heat.

In a large bowl, whisk together the egg yolks, vanilla bean seeds, orange zest, and salt until blended. Stream a ladle of the hot milk mixture into the egg yolks while whisking constantly to temper the yolks. Repeat with a couple of more ladles of hot milk, while whisking constantly. Pour the yolk mixture back into the pan and place over medium-low heat. Continue to heat, stirring constantly, until the mixture thickens enough to lightly coat the back of a spoon. Do not let the mixture begin to simmer or boil as you might end up with a scrambled-egg mixture that smells of wet dog.

Remove the pot from the heat and strain through a fine-mesh sieve (preferably lined with a coffee filter to result in an extra-silky premiun nog) into a clean heatproof bowl. Stir in the cream and finally the booze. Some like rum, some go whiskey, my mom prefers vodka—the choice is yours! Cover and chill before serving.

To serve, ladle the eggnog into cups and grate whole nutmeg and cinnamon stick vigorously over each filled cup. Make sure to place the extra nutmeg into your pocket for good luck.

SNACK
PARTY

Many times, the most wondrous and
elaborate outcomes are generated
by tiny, subtle beginnings.

FFFUN DIP

■ **MAKES ABOUT 2 CUPS**

Known to many out there—especially those in the Midwest—as Jarlsberg dip, this is a dish we couldn't resist renaming because it tastes much more fun than the word *Jarlsberg* could ever lead you to believe. A true crowd-pleaser, it perplexes folks who have never experienced it before. When served with the perfectly crunchy accompaniment like pretzels, it is seriously addictive stuff.

Throughout the years, we have experimented with different cheeses as the base and different toppings. Though all of the iterations have been delicious, with contrasting flavors of sweet and salty, there is something about the sweet, mild flavor of Jarlsberg that remains our favorite. The mix-ins are best when kept simple: a little acid, a lotta mayo, and a bit of good red onion or shallot. We have found that macerating the onion or shallot beforehand in some lemon juice, salt, and sugar allows the dip to age more gracefully in the refrigerator without getting too pungent with onion.

This dip should be proudly displayed with a flourish of honey-brined pickles and crunchy and sturdy dippers. A drizzle of spicy honey over the top and copious amounts of sliced scallions make it complete. Once you've made this dip, we promise you'll wish you had doubled the recipe.

¼ cup minced red onion or shallot

Fresh lemon juice, for macerating and seasoning

Kosher salt

Pinch of sugar

8–10 oz Jarlsberg cheese, shredded on the thinnest holes of a box grater

½ cup or so Hellmann's or Best Foods mayonnaise

Honey pickles (page 225), for garnish

Hot honey, for drizzling

Extra-virgin olive oil, for drizzling

Maldon or other crunchy salt, for finishing

Freshly ground black pepper, for garnish

Sliced green onions, white and green parts, for garnish

In a small bowl, combine the red onion, lemon juice to cover, a pinch of kosher salt, and the sugar, stir briefly, and then let sit for 15 minutes or so. Drain off the liquid, pressing against the red onion a bit to remove as much moisture as possible.

In a bowl, mix together the red onion mixture and cheese and then fold together with the mayonnaise. Add some lemon juice and season with kosher salt and pepper; taste and adjust if needed. Let sit for 15–20 minutes before serving. At this point, the dip can be covered and refrigerated for up to 2 days; bring to room temperature before serving.

To serve, scoop the dip onto a serving platter and make a well in the center. Scatter the pickles around in neat but loose piles. Garnish with a drizzle of hot honey, some great olive oil, crunchy salt, and a hefty dose of pepper, then let it rain with the green onions.

VARIATION

For our second, favorite version of this dip, we swap out the Jarlsberg for a high-quality Cheddar, like the outstanding Cheddar made by Vermont's Shelburne Farms. Everything else is the same except we trade out the pickles for chopped pepperoncini and the honey for a drizzle of *real* dark maple syrup. This version is best served with extra-dark, extra-crunchy pretzels.

MARTHA'S CARROTS

■ SERVES 6

Food has the power to ignite the gathering of people as well as their memories. After all, family recipes are just memories written down to be re-created in the form of food. Here is a favorite from Martha Barker, my husband, John's, grandmother. Visits to her home were always centered around family and food. Her cooking ability was known to be modest, but she always put out an impressive spread for even the shortest of visits. Her menus consisted of simple things like green salads, boiled potatoes, salmon cakes, and these famous fried carrots, which were always followed by her signature cinnamon rolls for dessert. While these carrots are a uniquely Martha preparation, John re-created this recipe through his memory because she never wrote it down. They are like baby carrot pancakes.

FOR THE BATTER

1 cup all-purpose flour

1 teaspoon baking powder

Kosher salt

1 cup milk, plus 1–2 tablespoons more if batter is too thick

1 large egg plus 1 large egg white

2 tablespoons bacon fat or butter, melted, plus more, unmelted, for frying

1 tablespoon apple cider vinegar

A few tablespoons of minced chives (optional)

—

6 medium carrots

1 lemon, halved, for serving (optional)

Aioli (page 81), for serving (optional)

HOT TIP This batter also makes exceptional pancakes for breakfast.

To make the batter, in a medium bowl, mix together the flour, baking powder, and 1 teaspoon salt. Add the milk, whole egg, egg white, bacon fat, vinegar, and chives (if using), and stir until a pancake-like batter forms.

Have ready a large bowl of ice water. Line a plate with a paper towel. Cut the carrots into 3-inch sections and then halve lengthwise. (They should be roughly ½ inch thick.) Bring a pot of salted water to a boil and cook the carrots for 5–6 minutes or until fork tender then shock in the ice bath until completely cooled. Transfer to the prepared plate to dry.

Place a cast-iron skillet over medium heat and melt some bacon fat. Line a plate with a paper towel. Dip the carrot pieces into the batter, coating well, and place in the skillet to fry. Once bottoms have turned a golden brown, flip them over to cook the other side. Once the other side is fully cooked and golden brown, move them to the prepared plate and season with salt. Let cool slightly and enjoy with a squeeze of lemon, dipped in aioli, or on their own.

LETTUCE CUPS WITH HERBY SPRING PEAS & GOAT CHEESE

■ **SERVES 12**

Peas usher in the first glimpse of spring. Their season is short where we live, so we try to celebrate them as much as possible. The initial harvest is so petite and tender, there is hardly any need to subject them to heat. The peas become sweeter at their peak and then more fibrous as the season winds down. We use these older, more fibrous peas differently than the young, tender ones, often reserving them for soups. Depending on where your peas are in this life cycle, you may need to give them a quick blanch or they might be delicious raw. Take a bite of a raw one and you'll know immediately what to do. The marinade used here is equally delicious on asparagus spears, leeks, and baby broccoli, all served blanched and prepared the same way. The goat cheese can be swapped out for ricotta or left out entirely for a dairy-free version.

FOR THE PEAS

Kosher salt and freshly ground black pepper

2 lb English shelling peas or sugar snap peas

Grated zest and juice of 2 large lemons and 1 large orange

2–3 cloves garlic, chopped

1–2 spring onions, julienned or thinly sliced on a mandoline

Handful of fresh flat-leaf parsley leaves, cut into chiffonade

Handful of fresh mint leaves, cut into chiffonade

Handful of fresh basil leaves, cut into chiffonade

½ cup fruity and buttery extra-virgin olive oil

Pinch of red chile flakes

Maldon salt

FOR THE WHIPPED GOAT CHEESE

1 lb plain chèvre (fresh goat cheese), at room temperature

¼ cup extra-virgin olive oil

Touch of heavy cream

—

4 heads Little Gem lettuce

To make the peas, have ready a large bowl of ice water. Bring a large pot filled with water to a boil over high heat. Season it liberally with kosher salt until it tastes like the sea. Drop the peas into the boiling water and cook until just slightly tender, about 1 minute. Scoop them out with a slotted spoon and immediately plunge them into the ice bath to cool.

Meanwhile, separate the leaves of the Little Gem heads, clean them, and gently pat dry. Set aside for serving.

Once the peas have chilled out a bit, drain them and give them a pat dry. Slice the peas into bite-size strips on the diagonal and transfer to a bowl.

In a small bowl, combine the lemon and orange zest and juice, garlic, onions, parsley, mint, basil, olive oil, chile flakes, 1 heaping tablespoon of Maldon salt, and a few twists of pepper and mix well. Pour over the peas and toss gently to mix well.

To make the whipped goat cheese, in a bowl, using an electric mixer or a whisk, whip together the cheese, oil, and cream until smooth and light. Season with kosher salt and pepper.

To assemble the dish, dollop a bit of the goat cheese mixture into each lettuce cup. Using a slotted spoon, top each one with a spoonful of the peas, then drizzle a little of the marinade over each one. Finish with a sprinkle of Maldon salt. Arrange on a platter and serve.

Note: This can also be served as a composed salad.

BAKED BLOOMY RIND CHEESE
WITH HABANADA JAM, ROASTED SHALLOTS & CRISPY PEPPERONI

- ■ SERVES 4–6 NICELY

Habanada peppers are a favorite on the farm. They are a heatless version of the habanero chile, which is a chile with such intense heat that you can barely taste its fruity flavors. The bloomy rind cheese family may have originated in France, but nowadays, positively exceptional members of the clan are made by small producers right here in the United States, and visiting a local farmers' market or cheesemonger can open up your knowledge to all the cheeses around you. We love serving a puck of one of these local bloomy gems in a cast-iron skillet with our fruity Habanada Jam baked on top. And if all you have floating around in your cheese drawer is a basic Brie, by all means whip it out. The gooey, fatty cheese and sweet, vibrant habanada preserves are made only better by the addition of crispy, salty pepperoni. Need I say more?

**Extra-virgin olive oil,
for the pan or dish**

**One 6–8-oz wheel double or
triple cream bloomy rind or
washed rind cheese**

**1 cup roughly chopped shallots,
gently sweated in butter or
olive oil until soft**

½ cup Habanada Jam (page 226)

**Fresh thyme or other hard
herb sprigs, for the pan or dish
(optional)**

**1 cup pepperoni slices
(preferably Ezzo brand)**

**Maldon salt and freshly ground
black pepper**

**Fresh thyme leaves,
for garnishing**

Potato chips, for serving

HOT TIP A very dry ricotta or a mild cow's milk feta is also good prepared this way.

Preheat the oven to 400°F.

Pick out a cast-iron pan or ceramic baking dish that just fits your cheese. Pour a small amount of oil onto the bottom and then place the cheese in the center. Top the cheese with the shallots, the jam, the pepperoni, and a sprinkle of salt.

Bake the cheese until it is bubbly, about 20 minutes. Remove from the oven and top with a bit of fresh thyme and a sprinkle of black pepper. Serve immediately with a large bowl of kettle potato chips (we like Cape Cod).

BAGNA CÀUDA

- **SERVES 4–6**

Every year in mid-October, we prepare the ground to receive thousands of garlic cloves that will grow into plump heads to harvest the following year. Because of the sheer number of cloves, this planting is always a full team effort. Many hands make light work and the task is complete in about two hours. Once we've finished, we head back to the barn kitchen to make a pot of bagna càuda with the remaining cloves that didn't quite make the cut. We enjoy it with an array of our fall vegetables and freshly baked bread while celebrating the end of a hot season of hard work.

A classic dish of the Piedmont region of northwestern Italy, bagna càuda is a warm and potent dip originally made by the local farmers to celebrate the autumn harvest. It calls for an obscene amount of both anchovies and garlic to ensure the boldest flavor, and must be prepared slowly, with patience, to ensure a good result. The highest-quality olive oil–packed anchovies must always be used, because the better the anchovy, the less fishy the dip! The poorer the quality, the more likely you are to end up with disturbing results. Understood?

Traditionally served as a communal dish, bagna càuda should be kept warm over a small flame at the table and accompanied with vegetables and crusty bread for dipping. The vegetables should be selected thoughtfully, as their sweetness or bitterness will play with the warm butter bath in different ways. They should be cut into manageable, attractive pieces for dipping and nibbling. Sweet red peppers, bitter chicories, lightly blanched cruciferous vegetables, celery ribs, and small fennel wedges are all good choices. Hard-boiled eggs, roasted potatoes, and sweet onion petals are also great.

---

1 cup heavy cream

24 cloves garlic, peeled

1 heaping cup well-drained oil-packed anchovy fillets

1 cup or so extra-virgin olive oil

½ cup (1 stick) or so great butter

Trimmed vegetables (see headnote) and crusty bread for dipping

Handful of fresh flat-leaf parsley alongside, for munching

In a small-to-medium, heavy saucepan, combine the cream and garlic cloves and poach over low heat until the cloves soften, 5–7 minutes. Add the anchovies and continue to cook, smashing everything together into a cohesive mash. Add the oil and butter and continue to cook until the garlic, anchovy, and milk solids look like sludge, about 25 minutes longer.

Remove from the heat, transfer to a serving bowl, and serve right away with the accompaniments. Any leftover dip can be stored in an airtight container in the refrigerator for up to 2 weeks.

THINGS TO TRY!

Add toasted and smashed hazelnuts to the dip just before serving, or substitute hazelnut oil for some of the olive oil.

Add a few spoonfuls of roasted cherry tomatoes (page 149) to the pot at the last minute and stir them until they begin to break apart.

Reheat gently and drizzle over sliced peak-season tomatoes or pizza.

HONEY WHIPPED TAHINI WITH DUKKAH

■ MAKES ABOUT 2 CUPS

This dip is a crowd-pleaser that accommodates many dietary restrictions. It can be made thicker or thinner depending on its intended use—thicker is great for a dip or sandwich spread, while thinner is best for dressing roasted fall roots, hearty greens, or slaws. Thinned out with more lemon juice and a bit of maple syrup, it is perfect for dressing a roasted fall root vegetable or cabbage slaw.

The quality of the tahini you use for this recipe is key—not all tahini is created equal, and many have bitter, off-putting flavors on the back of the palate. Our favorite is Soom, a Philadelphia-based company started by three sisters. We have been ecstatic fans for many years and think they produce the best tahini you can find in the US. We love to finish this dip off with a dusting of dukkah, a traditional Egyptian condiment of nuts, seeds, and spices that makes an ideal topper for nearly anything. Make sure to sprinkle liberally!

½ cup runny honey

Juice of 1–2 lemons

2 cloves garlic

1 cup high-quality tahini, well stirred until smooth

Kosher salt

Pinch of hot paprika or cayenne pepper

Up to 1 cup water

Trimmed vegetables, for dipping

FOR THE DUKKAH

About 1 cup peeled hazelnuts

About 1 cup shelled pistachios

½ cup or so sesame seeds

2 heaping tablespoons cumin seeds

2 heaping tablespoons coriander seeds

1 teaspoon aniseeds

½ cup or so unsweetened dried coconut flakes

2 tablespoons Maldon salt

In a food processor, combine the honey, lemon juice, and garlic then blitz until smooth. Add the tahini, 1 tablespoon kosher salt, and hot paprika and process until well mixed. You will notice the tahini will begin to seize up into a very thick mass. Do not fret! Drizzle in some water until it reaches a smooth, creamy, and airy consistency that will begin to take on a pearly sheen. Continue to process until the tahini holds a soft peak. Give it a taste and adjust the seasoning with more salt and lemon juice if needed.

Transfer to an airtight container and refrigerate for at least an hour or so before serving. It will firm up a good deal as it sits and chills and can always be thinned out with a touch more water. It will keep in the refrigerator for up to 2 weeks. When ready to serve, spoon into a bowl or swoosh a thick smear of it on a platter, arrange the vegetables around, and dust with the dukkah.

To make the dukkah, preheat the oven to 350°F. Spread the hazelnuts and pistachios on a small sheet pan and toast, stirring once or twice, until golden brown and aromatic, 7–10 minutes. Pour onto a plate and let cool.

In a skillet, combine the sesame seeds, cumin seeds, coriander seeds, and aniseeds and toast over medium heat, shaking the pan often to prevent burning, until they darken slightly and are fragrant, 3–4 minutes. Toss in the coconut at the last minute to get it a tad golden. Pour on a plate to cool.

Once everything is at room temperature, transfer the nuts and seeds to a food processor and pulse until the mixture is at the desired consistency. Pour into a small bowl and stir in the Maldon salt. Transfer to an airtight container and store in a cool cupboard. It will keep for up to 2 weeks.

GREEN GARLIC & ALMOND DIP

■ MAKES ABOUT 2 CUPS

Green garlic is always a glory to work with in the kitchen. This technically immature garlic is bright and gentle in flavor, a reminder that the hard work done in the field the previous fall was well worth the effort. Green garlic is harvested before the bulb fully develops and cures into papery white heads. It has a much purer and sweeter flavor than its cured version, though it's still pungent. If you aren't able to find green garlic but are making recipes that call for it, use a combination of leeks and garlic. You can also poach cured garlic cloves in a bit of milk for a few minutes to mellow their flavor.

Both sweet and savory items pair well with this dip. We love serving it with grapes and pear wedges, Little Gems or other petite lettuce leaves, blanched sugar snap peas, cooked new potatoes, spears of cucumber and carrot, and turnip wedges. Complete the spread with a bowl of fancy potato chips.

---

1 cup peeled almonds,
such as Marcona

4–6 cloves green garlic,
depending on taste, pungency,
and size

Some garlic scapes (optional)

½ cup ice-cold water,
plus more as needed

1–2 slices white bread,
crusts removed, torn

½ cup extra-virgin olive oil

Splash of vinegar, such as
white wine, champagne, sherry,
or moscatel, or fresh lemon juice

Kosher salt

Pinch of red chile flakes

2 tablespoons runny honey
or agave nectar

In a food processor, combine the almonds, green garlic, garlic scapes (if using), and ice water and process until everything breaks down and the mixture becomes creamy, adding a little more water if needed to help it along. Add the bread, oil, and vinegar and let the machine run until the mixture has a creamy, airy consistency, thinning it out with more water or vinegar if needed. Toss in a couple of pinches of salt, the chile flakes, and the honey, processing again until smooth. Taste and adjust the seasoning if needed.

Transfer the dip to an airtight container and refrigerate for an hour or so to set up before serving. It will keep in the refrigerator for up to 1 week.

RADISHES WITH BUTTER & HONEY

■ SERVES 4–6

Rarely has a butter come around that I have not loved, and the same goes for a radish! Put the two together and you have a simple snack for a picnic or a dish elegant enough to sit next to caviar. It truly is a classic combination that stands the test of time. I love making this dish in late spring, when the radishes are petite, sweet, and contain just a dash of heat, or in the fall once the weather cools down and their sugar content increases to bring out juicy, almost fruity flavors. Radishes worthy for this dish do not come in the water-soaked bags perched next to the weird baby carrots at the supermarket. Visit your local farmers' market or co-op grocery store for freshly pulled roots with their perky tops still attached or grow a little plot of your own! Baby turnips like the snow-white Japanese Hakurei variety are a delicious substitution if radishes are not available.

Few bunches of the best radishes you can find

½ lb European-style butter, at room temperature

Maldon or other crunchy finishing salt

Runny honey, for drizzling

Extra-virgin olive oil, for drizzling

HOT TIP Source the best butter you can find, always looking for a higher fat content (85%) or cultured or European-style butter. These are packed with tangy, deep grassy flavors much like a cheese.

Clean the radishes, leaving the tops on if they are bright and perky, and give them a pat dry. If the radishes are on the large size, cut them into pretty shapes, making sure the pieces are not too thin or they will snap when dragged through the butter.

On your serving plate or board, create a swoosh with the butter and arrange the radishes about it. Sprinkle the butter and radishes with a bit of salt and then drizzle with the honey and oil.

CHARRED VEGETABLES WITH ROMESCO

- **SERVES 6–8**

A classic sauce from Catalonia, romesco is smoky, sweet, and flavorful and is wonderful served with grilled vegetables, seafood, sandwiches, and eggs. It also happens to be one of the best ways to feature our farm's sweet and meaty red peppers and our most prized onions: Tropeana Lunga, a torpedo-shaped red-pink Italian variety high in sugar and with the most intoxicating flavor. To showcase the beauty of these heirloom onions, we like to leave them whole and lay them over wood-fired coals to cook slowly before draping them over the savory sauce.

Traditionally, romesco includes bread crumbs to give the sauce added body and texture. We generally like to treat the classics as inspiration, so here we make ours a robust gluten-free version that works for almost any gathering. In addition to nearly any charred vegetables that appeal—from summer squashes and broccoli to leeks and cauliflower—proteins like grilled chicken, pork, or prawns dunked in garlic butter are also superb laid over a pool of romesco. Finally, a consistent flow of wine to accompany the cooking and eating of this grand dish is a must!

FOR THE ROMESCO

2–3 cups freshly roasted red sweet peppers with their skins, seeds, and stems removed

1 heaping cup mixed toasted nuts, such as almonds, hazelnuts, pine nuts, and walnuts

3–4 cloves garlic, grated

1 medium-hot fresh red chile, such as a Fresno or serrano, stemmed and seeded if desired

½ cup extra-virgin olive oil

Few splashes of aged sherry vinegar

Grated zest and juice of 1 orange

Grated zest and juice of 1 lemon

1 tablespoon sweet or hot smoked paprika

Dollop of runny honey

Kosher salt

—

Vegetables of choice, for grilling

Extra-virgin olive oil, for coating and for finishing

Kosher salt

Torn fresh herb leaves of choice, for garnish

To make the romesco, in a food processor, combine the peppers, nuts, garlic, chile, oil, vinegar, citrus zest and juice, paprika, honey, and a big pinch of salt and blitz everything until well combined but still slightly textured. Taste and adjust with acid, honey, and salt to make the sauce perfectly balanced and sultry.

Prepare a grill for direct-heat cooking over a medium-hot fire.

While the grill is getting nice and hot, ready your vegetables, trimming and cutting them as needed and setting them aside on a sheet pan as they are ready. Coat the vegetables with oil and season them with salt.

When the grill is ready, char the vegetables directly over the fire, turning as needed, until cooked through and nicely charred but not overdone.

Spoon the sauce onto a large platter and arrange the vegetables over the sauce. The dish is complete with a drizzle of oil—ideally a Spanish olive oil—and a scattering of herbs.

FRESH HERBS RULE!

Any person who intends to cook well must have access to fresh herbs. They will be the key that takes a creation to the next level. Our cooking would be a shell of what it is without them. Bunches of flowering herbs adorn our kitchen counters and tablescapes, to pluck at arm's reach, to complete everything from dainty starters to bowls of ice cream.

Over time, herbs seem to have convinced generations that they only go with certain foods: mint with lamb, basil with tomatoes, and thyme with mushrooms. This was decided by one person, at one point in time, and a few others agreed. How crazy is that?!

While these have become "traditional" flavor pairings, they also happen to be absolute superstition. Fresh herbs should encourage experimentation rather than restriction. Believing that specific herbs are only suited for specific dishes is utterly arbitrary. Such partnerships should be judged only by personal taste.

For example, basil works wonderfully to bring out the flavor of most anything it touches. It is just as well suited to guacamole or a dessert as it is to a tomato salad. Freshly budded marjoram is glorious scattered over roasted beets, rolled into meat, or even dabbed on the wrist when a touch of "perfume" is needed. Mint can be used to give a clean taste and vibrant tang to cocktails, salads, and braised meat. Some herbs, such as sage and rosemary, have a pervasive nature and need to be used with a lighter hand. They can be magical when used in the right amount, but when used incorrectly, they are a total turnoff.

The harvest age of fresh herbs affects their flavor. Some softer herbs, like parsley, dill, and mint, can become bitter and unpalatable if left to grow too large, while others, like cilantro, become even more wonderful when left to blossom.

We often call for "torn herbs" in recipes because we find that knives, especially dull ones, damage the oils in the leaves. Tearing the leaves gives a casual, more sensual quality to a dish, allowing the oils to be released freshly into the mouth. When taking a blade to an herb, make sure it is sharp. Otherwise, you will end up with a muddy chlorophyll mush.

Herbs have their limits when it comes to heat. Their oils break down and evaporate quickly when exposed to heat, and peak flavor is drawn out after about 20 minutes of cook time. If left to cook too long, herbs tend to make a dish dull rather than bright. And forget about dried herbs! They turn most dishes into an utter waste. Their oils change in the drying process, and their flavors become flat and musty. They ought to be labeled "sawdust."

If you attempt to grow one thing at your home, let it be fresh herbs. Without a doubt, you will get the most value back for both time and money spent, and your dishes will set your palate free! You will never consider reaching for jars of tired dried herbs in your pantry again.

THE HUMBLE DEVILED EGG

■ MAKES 12

Deviled eggs are the retro nostalgic bite that are often the first thing to be devoured at a gathering. I refer to the recipe as humble because these deviled eggs are built on a solid, simple foundation—protein-packed bites whipped together with everyday ingredients. But when made with top-notch eggs and executed at a high level, they are not so humble anymore. Instead, they become creamy, dense, and unctuous nuggets of luxury. Add a reasonable garnish—a sliver of crunchy bacon, a caper or two, a dollop of fish roe—and nothing more, to keep the flavors and texture pure and true.

Some insist that older eggs are best for hard boiling, claiming they are easier to peel. I find the exact opposite to be true. We use the freshest eggs we can find, usually from the hens on our farm.

However old or new your eggs are, a word of advice: allow for disasters to occur because they will. One dozen eggs can turn into three, and your kitchen sink could soon become an eggshell demolition zone. This recipe makes a dozen deviled eggs, but I suggest boiling a few extra because one or two will inevitably shit the bed.

Should you not have sympathy, patience, or time for the devil, this recipe can be turned into a bangin' egg salad. Simply give a rough chop to the peeled whole boiled eggs, toss them with the remaining ingredients, and serve on buttered warm toast with leaves of peppery arugula and bits of crispy bacon.

---

6 large eggs, plus a few extra in case of cracks

¼ cup or so high-quality mayonnaise

Knob of room-temperature butter (about 1 tablespoon)

2 teaspoons Dijon mustard

¼ cup or so mixed minced fresh herbs (such as tarragon, flat-leaf parsley, and chives), green onion, and shallot

Juice of 1 lemon, or 1–2 dashes of white wine vinegar

Pinch of cayenne pepper

Kosher salt and freshly ground black pepper

Garnish of choice
(see Variations)

Grab a pot that will accommodate your eggs in a single layer. (If you are boiling many eggs, work in batches.) Place the eggs in the pot, fill it gently with enough water to cover the eggs by about 2 inches, and then carefully remove the eggs. Place the pot over high heat and bring the water to a boil. Gently lower the eggs into the water, reduce the heat slightly, and simmer for exactly 11 minutes. If an egg cracks, don't fret! Just replace it with another.

While the eggs are simmering, fill a large bowl with ice water and set it near the stove. The moment the egg timer goes off, carefully spoon the eggs into the ice bath for a cool plunge while you gather the rest of the ingredients.

If you are using very fresh eggs, this technique should make peeling easy: Tap each egg on its butt (where the air pocket forms when cooking) and then, holding the egg under running cool water, peel off the shell. Give a final rinse to the fully peeled egg to rid it of all shell debris.

Once you've peeled all the eggs, slice them in half lengthwise, wiping the knife clean after each slice and popping the yolks out into a bowl. Place the hollowed-out whites on a kitchen towel to absorb any excess water.

VARIATIONS

Garnish: Sliver or two of raw or pickled vegetable, 1 or 2 capers, fresh herb leaf, crispy bacon sliver, pinch of toasted garlic panko, dot of hot sauce, slice of anchovy fillet, dollop of fish roe, shaving of white truffle.

Curry: Add 1 heaping teaspoon hot curry powder to the yolk mixture. Garnish each deviled egg with a small dice of sharp white onion.

Mash the yolks with a fork until they are more or less smooth. Add the mayonnaise, butter, and mustard and continue to mash and mix to smooth the yolks. Add the herb mixture, lemon juice, and cayenne pepper, season with salt and black pepper, and mix well. Taste and then tweak the mixture until it suits your palate.

Stuff each egg half with the yolk mixture, using a spoon for a more casual presentation or a piping bag with a star or round tip for a more refined appearance. Garnish with any fun bits you like, but don't overload them. Serve right away.

SLOW-ROASTED GARLIC
WITH BLUE CHEESE & FIG PRESERVES

- **SERVES 4–6**

Billowing bonfires with crackling wood, a crisp, sweet breeze carrying leaves at the end of their life cycle, wafts of jammy red wine and burnt toast, and garlic slowly roasting in fat—these are a few of my favorite smells.

3–4 heads garlic

Extra-virgin olive oil

Maldon salt

Soft, creamy blue cheese with not too much bite, such as Saint Agur or Gorgonzola dolce

Fig preserves or runny honey

Chewy sourdough baguette

HOT TIP The foil-wrapped garlic can instead be cooked over hot coals.

Preheat the oven to 400°F.

Peel away and discard any loose, papery skins from the garlic heads but keep the heads intact. Slice the tips off each garlic head, exposing the ends of the cloves for easy squeezing later on. Lay a piece of aluminum foil on a sheet pan and place the garlic heads, root side down, on the center of the foil. Top each head with a drizzle of oil and a sprinkle of salt, then cover the heads with the edges of the foil, making a neat little knapsack.

Bake the garlic until it is soft to the touch and the sugars within have caramelized to a golden brown, 40–60 minutes.

Arrange the garlic heads on a platter or board and place the creamy blue cheese and a pot of fig preserves alongside.

Invite guests to dress pieces of torn baguette with a swipe of cheese, a squeeze of a clove, and a dollop of preserves. Serve with a lightly chilled red or sparkling Lambrusco on a crisp fall day—ah, simple things.

SNACKING PEPPERS

■ SERVES 4–6

Snacking peppers have become much more widely known and popular over recent years in the US but have been on menus for quite some time in Spain, Japan, and South Korea. Petite and neither too sweet nor too hot, they are typically quickly cooked or blistered in a skillet with hot oil or over the open flame of a grill and then consumed in a single bite as an accompaniment to a cold beer or a glass of wine. Occasionally you might come across one or two with a spark of heat, but generally they contain very little to none.

We have grown many different varieties of snacking peppers over the years, from the Spanish Padrón to the Japanese shishito and Fushimi. In more recent years, a new variety, the Habanada, has become one of our favorites to use for this preparation as well as for jam (page 226). A wedge of lemon, a bit of aioli, and Maldon salt really set these babies off in an addictive way that will make you always want to go back for more. Have your friends gather around you while you're cooking the peppers so they can eat them the moment they are ready—and have plenty of cold beer ready too.

Neutral oil with a high smoke point, such as grapeseed or canola, for frying

2–3 quarts snacking peppers, such as Padrón, shishito, or Habanada, with stems intact

Few lemon or lime cheeks, for garnish

Maldon salt

Aioli of choice (pages 81–83), for serving (optional)

HOT TIP For a fun variation, top with toasted sesame seeds and wispy bonito flakes or fried and salted Marcona almonds.

Place a cast-iron skillet or other shallow, heavy pan over high heat on your stove top or grill. Drizzle in a bit of neutral oil. When the oil is nearly smoking, toss in a handful of peppers in a single layer, being careful not to crowd them in the pan. Crowding these little buggers will cause them to steam, leaving them to become overcooked mush, so cook them in small batches. Give the peppers a shake and a toss with some tongs until they have little caramel-toned blisters on all sides.

Arrange them in a pile on a board or platter with a few lemon cheeks on the side. Bless with a shower of salt and serve a ramekin of aioli on the side for dipping, if you wish. Serve up each batch as soon as it's ready.

PADRÓN

LE GRAND AÏOLI

■ SERVES AS MANY AS YOU WISH

A classic of Provence, le grand aïoli is a feast of raw and blanched vegetables proudly displayed around the region's classic sauce, aioli. Lightly steamed seafood, tinned food, and slices of charcuterie are also welcomed in the creation of this platter. It is a low-key yet dramatic dish that is as much a feast for the eyes as for the mouth. All in all, it is a quite elegant meal for any time of day or occasion. It can be prepared in advance, which makes it a decidedly relaxing choice for the cook or host. A fair warning—having a back stock for replenishing trays and platters as the bits get devoured is a must. Although nothing pairs better with a trimmed-up farmers' market haul than a rich and pungent aioli, it of course can be swapped out for any of the other dips or creamy dressings in this book and beyond. Serving more than one dip is wildly appropriate too!

Now let's talk about how to nail it. Buy a vivid mixture of in-season produce and take the time to peel, trim, cut up, and blanch everything yourself. Yes, this will take some time, but the result is well worth the effort. Don't you dare look at those plastic-covered trays of precut vegetables in the grocery store! Arrange the produce in tidy, casual bundles around your dips of choice. Add accents and fill in any gaps with contrasting items until you can no longer see your serving vessel. Sturdy petite lettuce leaves, hard-boiled eggs, simply boiled new potatoes, chilled seafood, tins of fish, olives, and sliced meats—all are welcome, and abundance is key. Decorate with edible garnishes like flowering herbs, salted nuts, dried legumes, and perhaps even some pickles. Everything, aside from the chilled seafood, is best served at room temperature so all the beautiful flavors can be fully appreciated.

Next, just add a joyous group of people with clean hands to participate, as utensils are a sin! Le grand aïoli can be offered as an appetizer at a party for many or as a luxurious main course for two. No matter how you serve it, it should always be eaten with leisure accompanied by ample amounts of chilled wine. On our farm, aioli is in full bloom 365 days a year. This Provençal egg-based delight transforms the most mundane dishes to imaginative masterpieces. Best served with meat, seafood, or vegetables, aioli can be used as a condiment, ingredient, or spread.

6–10 cloves young, very fresh garlic

2 large whole eggs

2 large egg yolks

Juice of 1–2 lemons

Kosher salt

3 cups neutral oil, such as grapeseed, or half extra-virgin olive oil and half grapeseed for more punch

Water, as needed

Using a Microplane or other fine-rasp grater, grate the garlic—use more or fewer cloves according to your taste or your garlic—directly into the bowl of a food processor. Add the whole eggs, egg yolks, lemon juice—again, more or less to taste—and a hefty pinch of salt. Blitz all of this together for a few seconds. Then, with the processor running, add a few drops of oil. (I like to use a squeeze bottle for the best control over tiny drops.) The mixture will begin to emulsify within a few moments, becoming a bit tacky and thick. Once it has emulsified, you can stream in the oil at a faster pace. When the mixture is extremely thick and sticky, add a bit of water and mix until creamy and lush. Taste and adjust the seasoning with more salt or lemon juice. The aioli should be punchy and intense with more flavor than you think it may need. Devour right away or transfer to an airtight container and store in the refrigerator for up to 1 week.

Recipe continues

HOT TIPS

This recipe yields a little over 4 cups and serves ten to twelve nicely—unless you're like me and prefer all your food to come with a bowl of aioli on the side. Should you not have twelve guests to indulge, it is still a good idea to make the full amount. Just keep the remainder in the refrigerator for a midnight snack. Or play with different variations by dividing a batch into two or three portions and flavor each differently, whisking a minced fresh herb into one, a little chile powder into another, or whatever you like. Always be sure to use the highest-quality and freshest eggs you can find.

For an ultra-tight aioli, chill the processor bowl and blade and the ingredients well before you begin, to help strengthen the emulsification.

My preferred way to make aioli is actually by hand with a mortar and pestle.

VARIATIONS

Spicy: Follow the basic recipe, adding about 2 teaspoons cayenne pepper, more or less to taste, with the eggs. A drizzle of honey or a pinch of sugar to complement the heat can also be a nice touch.

Curry: Follow the basic recipe, substituting ¼ cup minced white onion for the garlic and adding 1–2 tablespoons curry powder, more or less to taste, and a pinch of sugar with the eggs. This makes a great accompaniment to steamed whole artichokes or fresh cracked crab.

Anchovy: Follow the basic recipe, adding 6–8 anchovy fillets in olive oil, more or less to taste, to the eggs and blitz to a fine paste. A pinch of cayenne pepper or paprika pairs well, or you can fold in a bit of minced fresh flat-leaf parsley at the end for an herbaceous punch.

Pickled Pepper: Before making the aioli, chop up a couple of handfuls of pepperoncini or honey pickled peppers (page 225) and blitz in a food processor to a fine mash. When making the aioli, reduce the number of garlic cloves by about half and substitute the pickled pepper liquid for the lemon juice. Add a pinch of sugar with the garlic, eggs, and salt. Finish the aioli with more pickled pepper liquid or chopped peppers as needed.

Sherried: Follow the basic recipe, reducing the number of garlic cloves by half and swapping out the lemon juice for a nice aged sherry vinegar. Once the aioli is complete, mix in a few drops of a nutty sherry wine and a pinch of paprika.

California Style: Meyer lemons invoke memories and smells of California. This sauce is perfect with chilled seafood, blanched asparagus spears, or steamed artichokes. Chop up one Meyer lemon and discard its seeds and ends. Place it in a food processor with a small shallot, a bit of fresh chile, like Fresno or serrano, and a dash of moscato or rice wine vinegar. Pulse until a mash is formed and then toss in kosher salt and about ⅓ cup extra-virgin olive oil. Blend until pureed. It should yield close to a cup of puree. Fold this into a quart of basic aioli, depending on how lemony you want it. Finish by folding in finely chopped herbs such as parsley, chervil, tarragon, or chives.

OTHER AIOLI BASED SAUCES

Gribiche: Make the basic aioli recipe but eliminate the garlic. Replace the lemon juice with a few tablespoons of red wine vinegar and stir in a few spoonfuls of smooth Dijon mustard. Fold in a few tablespoons of coarsely chopped capers, and cornichons, minced shallot, and finely chopped herbs, such as parsley, tarragon, chervil, chives and/or dill. Lastly, chop up 4–6, peeled and cleaned hard-boiled eggs and fold them in with care. Season with kosher salt and a pinch of cayenne pepper.

Rouille: Addictive bliss! Take the basic aioli recipe and add in one medium roasted red pepper that has been cleaned of its seeds and skin when the garlic is added, along with a couple pinches of saffron threads. Toss in a few tablespoons of white bread crumbs and pulse the mixture. Add in the eggs and lemon juice, blending until smooth, then begin to emulsify with the oil. I like subbing out half the neutral oil for some extra-virgin olive oil for more flavor. Season with kosher salt and a pinch of smoked paprika or piment d'espelette.

Tonnato: A famous Italian sauce that makes everything taste better. Make a basic batch of aioli and reserve in a bowl. In a food processor, blitz 2–4 anchovies, a few tablespoons of drained capers, one can of quality oil-packed tuna, and zest from a lemon until mostly smooth. Add a few glugs of white wine vinegar to keep it all moving along. Add in about a cup or two of the aioli and mix until smooth, thinning out or thickening up as needed. Season with kosher salt.

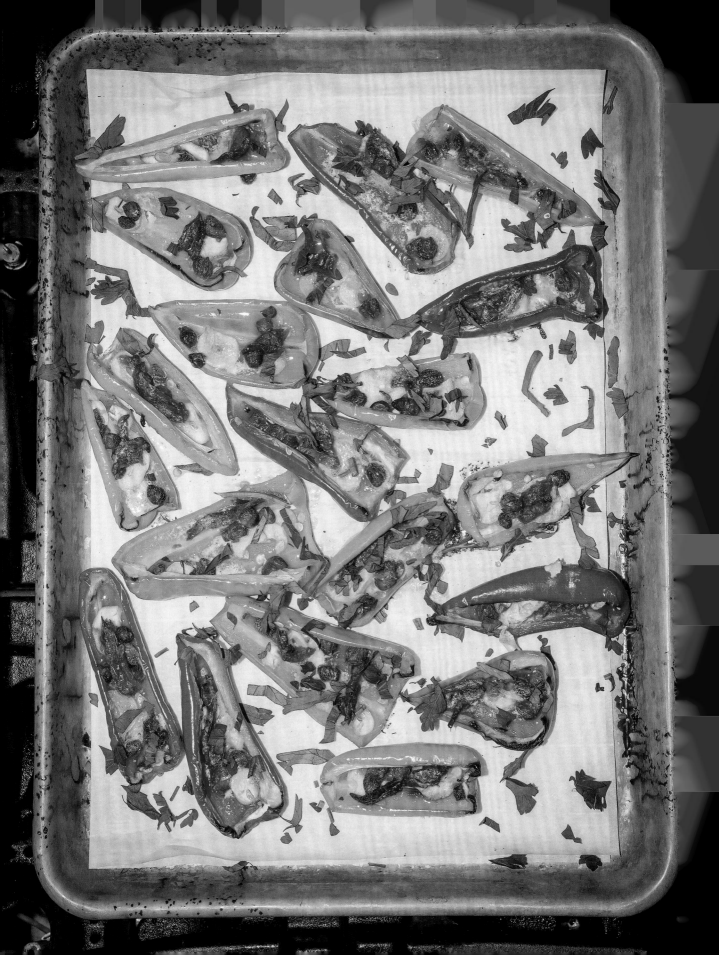

PARTY PEPPERS

The party version of the familiar stuffed pepper. It is hypnotizing, fatty, and laden with garlic—and, like most recipes in this book, it can be tweaked. Olives or capers can replace the anchovies for punchy salinity, and rosettes of ricotta can adorn the peppers once they have cooled to room temperature. Garnish them with flecks of citrus zest or torn herbs to make them pop for both the eyes and mouth.

Preheat the oven to 400°F. Line a sheet pan or baking dish with aluminum foil. Cut petite sweet peppers that are 2–3 inches long in half lengthwise. Discard the seeds and give the peppers a good rinse. Place a few slivers of garlic, a torn bit of anchovy fillet, and/or a sweet cherry tomato half, and a pea-size bit of butter into each pepper cavity. Drizzle with olive oil and sprinkle with kosher salt.

Arrange the stuffed pepper halves on the prepared pan and bake until the peppers are just tender, 15–17 minutes. Don't allow them to turn to mush. You want them to have some texture and be a bit al dente.

Top with toasted bread crumbs (page 115) for crunch or serve as is with a flurry of torn fresh flat-leaf parsley leaves. The peppers are best served at room temperature or slightly chilled.

HOT TIP To transform the peppers into an individually plated appetizer, serve a few in a shallow bowl nestled up against a cold hunk of burrata or buffalo mozzarella. Top with loads of torn fresh herb leaves and a drizzle of nice olive oil. Serve crusty bread on the side for mopping up the juices.

HOW TO TREAT AN OLIVE

Transforming these small, plump fruits into flavor bombs requires very little effort. They are the perfect fatty morsel to serve with a sunset cocktail or to kick off a dinner party. Olives with pits have better flavor and texture than ones with their pits removed. Get a mixture of buttery and briny types, such as Castelvetrano, Taggiasca, Cerignola, Niçoise, and/or Kalamata. These ingredients are easy to omit, substitute for, or add to, depending on what you have on hand, though I find fennel seeds and aniseeds impart particularly delicious flavors and should not be skipped.

2 cups assorted olives
2 cups extra-virgin olive oil, plus more as needed
Few cloves garlic, lightly smashed
1 fresh or dried whole chile, or pinch of red chile flakes
1–2 strips citrus zest of choice, removed with a vegetable peeler
1 heaping tablespoon fennel seeds
Pinch of aniseeds
2 bay leaves
Few fresh rosemary or thyme sprigs
Crusty bread, for serving

Divide the olives between 2 large jars.

In a small saucepan, combine the oil, garlic, chile, citrus zest, fennel seeds, aniseeds, and bay leaves over low heat and heat until the mixture becomes alluring and fragrant, about 5 minutes. Remove from the heat and pour the mixture over the olives in the jars. Top each jar with a touch more oil as needed to cover the olives, and cap with the lids. Store them for a good while in the refrigerator. The longer the olives sit in the jar, the more they will soak up the goodness that surrounds them, and the better they will taste.

To serve, preheat the oven to 320°F. Dump the olives and oil into a cast-iron skillet and add the rosemary. Place in the oven and heat gently until warmed through, about 15 minutes. Serve the olives directly from the pan with a small bowl on the side for the pits and a generous amount of bread for sopping up the oil.

ONION TEA SANDWICHES

- **SERVES 8–12**

Here is a little-known sandwich from the celebrated master himself, James Beard. Said to be one of his favorite snacks, it is simple, elegant, and super delicious. A humble sandwich that can be dressed up for the fanciest occasion or thrown together at a moment's notice to eat alone next to the kitchen sink.

Onions are among our most favorite things we grow on the farm, and this is a great way to celebrate their sweet arrival in spring. Sweeter onions, like Cippolini or baby Vidalia, are great used here.

When prepared in high fashion, the onion sandwich becomes a poetic juxtaposition of simple ingredients presented with flair. Enjoy with a very cold bottle of extra-brut Champagne.

---

1 loaf sliced white bread, such as pain de mie, brioche, shokupan (Japanese milk bread), or challah

1 cup or so aioli (page 81) or Kewpie brand mayonnaise

2 or more sweet onions, depending on size

Maldon salt and freshly ground black pepper

Finely chopped fresh soft herbs, such as chives, flat-leaf parsley, chervil, tarragon, and/or mint

6 hard-boiled egg yolks, sieved (see Hot Tip)

1/3 cup poppy seeds

Caviar, for serving

Gourmet potato chips, for serving

HOT TIP Hard boil the eggs, peel them, and separate the yolks from the whites. Have yourself a protein-packed snack of the whites while you press the yolks through a fine-mesh sieve, scraping the sieved yolks onto a sheet pan or sheet of parchment paper.

Slice the crusts off the bread and cut the slices into desired matching shapes, such as triangles, circles, or squares. Arrange them in pairs and spread each piece with aioli.

Using a mandoline or sharp knife, thinly slice the onions into rounds or half rounds. Place a few slices on half of the bread slices and top with a sprinkle of salt. Don't overload the bread. You want to keep these sandwiches on the dainty side. Top with the matching bread piece, aioli side down.

Have the chopped herbs, sieved yolks, and poppy seeds ready on a sheet pan or sheet of parchment paper. Spread some aioli on the edges of each sandwich, making clean swipes. Dip one aioli-coated side of the sandwich in the herbs and the other side in the egg yolks and poppy seeds—or coat however pleases you—and set aside on a platter.

The sandwiches can be served right away, or they can be covered and chilled for up to 2 hours before serving. Serve with a large ramekin of caviar, potato chips, and a nice Champagne or Sancerre.

BACON & COMPOUND BUTTER CROSTINI

■ SERVES AS MANY AS YOU WISH

Bacon and butter might seem a bit redundant, and that, my friend, is indeed the point! They are redundant and absolutely delicious together! Both are fatty and rich toppings that happen to pair magnificently on top of toasted bread to make a fantastic bite suitable for any season or occasion.

In England, this is a common snack known as a bacon butty, assembled on toasted white bread and dressed with a touch of ketchup in addition to the bacon and butter.

We find it the perfect use for a bold compound butter (pages 227–229) and play with the flavors in the butter as the seasons change. Different compound butters make the flavors pop in their own way: herbs and citrus give brightness, while smoked paprika or a touch of sherry lends a smoky richness.

The key to this bite is balance, which will allow the contrast of the ingredients to shine. All the toast needs is a confident swipe of butter, not a gloppy schmear.

The pork product should be cut thin and cooked extra crispy. Chewy, thick bacon isn't a wise or thoughtful decision here and won't be easy for your guests to bite into. The two ingredients should sit pretty together rather than compete with one another. Lastly, the bread should be very good, a nice, dense, and chewy country sourdough loaf or baguette ideally from a local bakery. Toast it well but only on one side to avoid turning it into sawdust.

Preheat the oven to 400°F. Line a sheet pan with parchment paper or aluminum foil and place a wire rack on top. Lay slices of bacon, pancetta, or guanciale neatly on the rack, being careful not to overload it. Bake until the bacon or other meat is like glass, about 15 minutes. Remove from the oven.

Preheat the broiler in your oven or, if outside, fire up the grill. Drizzle bread slices with olive oil. Give them a light char on the oiled side for a couple of minutes. Allow the bread to cool ever so slightly so the butter doesn't melt right away.

Spread the compound butter on each slice on the charred side and top with a crispy shard of bacon and perhaps a squeeze of lemon. Serve immediately with a glass of very cold Champagne or a chilled light red wine.

EGGPLANT CAPONATA

■ SERVES 8–10

Similar to ratatouille, this Sicilian eggplant dish is both sweet and sour and is a great way to utilize much of summer's bounty. Our version is loaded with produce that is prime on the farm when eggplant is ready for picking, such as summer squash and peppers. If you don't have the full gamut of produce listed here, feel free to omit a vegetable or two—but definitely not the eggplant!

We love taking a pint of this caponata along on picnics to accompany a spread of cheeses and charcuterie. It sings on a sandwich with slices of milky fresh mozzarella and fluffy oiled focaccia and is a wonderful room-temperature side to accompany roasted chicken or fish. It's also a great do-ahead dish—the flavors develop more after a day or two—and freezes well, so make a big batch when summer is in full swing. Garnish it simply with a drizzle of spicy olive oil, toasted pine nuts or almonds, and plenty of fresh parsley and basil. Voilà!

2–4 medium-size eggplants

2 summer squash

½ cup extra-virgin olive oil

1–2 yellow onions, finely diced

4–5 cloves garlic, chopped

3–4 celery ribs

2 sweet peppers, seeded and chopped

1–2 fresh chiles, chopped, or 2 pinches of red chile flakes

½ cup pine nuts

¼ cup raisins

Kosher salt

¼ cup or so tomato paste

½ cup or so tomato purée

1 heaping cup pitted green olives, such as Castelvetrano or Spanish

¼ cup capers

2 teaspoons unsweetened cocoa powder

1 teaspoon ground cinnamon

½ cup red wine vinegar

Grated zest and juice of 2 lemons

Generous drizzle of runny honey

1–2 pinches of dried oregano and dried thyme

Cut the eggplants and squash into bite-size cubes. In a large, wide, shallow pot or rondeau, heat the oil over medium heat. Toss in the onions, garlic, celery, sweet peppers, chiles, pine nuts, and raisins and season with a bit of salt to coax out their liquids. Sweat until fragrant, 8–10 minutes, and then add the eggplant and squash, sprinkle with a little salt (to extract their water), and cook, stirring often, until they have released some of their moisture and it has mostly evaporated, about 15 minutes more.

Make a well in the center of the pot, put the tomato paste into the well, and cook, stirring, until it turns a rusty hue. Add the tomato purée, olives, capers, cocoa powder, cinnamon, vinegar, lemon zest and juice, honey, and about 2 teaspoons salt. Stir everything together and add the oregano and thyme. Reduce the heat to low and cook, stirring occasionally, until the mixture thickens to a stew consistency. This should take 30–40 minutes. If the pan gets too dry, add a little bit of water or wine and continue to let the vegetables stew.

Taste and adjust any seasonings as needed. Let the caponata cool, then eat right away, transfer to an airtight container, or refrigerate for a day or two before serving. Store for up to 1 week in the refrigerator or freeze for up to 3 months.

MELTED BROCCOLI TOASTS

■ **MAKES ABOUT 2 QUARTS**

Let's label this "tastes better than it looks." It is nearly impossible to add acid to a green vegetable and not have it turn a putrid shade, but prolonged cooking with toasty garlic and olive oil mellows this cruciferous creature into broccoli bliss, so just trust me on this one.

It is addictively good served on top of oiled and toasted bread with a bit of black pepper and shavings of a salty firm cheese. Likewise, it makes for a wonderful pasta sauce or topping for a fried cutlet or on our Tarte Flambée (page 131). Served cold, it makes a divine sandwich spread to accompany thin shavings or roast pork or a chicken cutlet.

---

1 cup extra-virgin olive oil

2–3 heads garlic, cloves separated, peeled, and chopped

Pinch of red chile flakes, cayenne pepper, or finely chopped fresh chile

3–4 lb broccoli, florets and stems chopped into 2-inch pieces

About 3 cups water

1 heaping tablespoon kosher salt

Grated zest and juice of 2–3 lemons

Oiled and toasted sourdough baguette slices for serving

Garnish of choice

In a large, heavy pot, heat about ½ cup of the oil over medium heat, add the garlic and chile flakes, and cook, stirring occasionally, until the garlic is fragrant and slightly golden, 3–5 minutes. Add the broccoli, water, and salt, stir well, cover tightly, reduce the heat to medium-low, and simmer until the broccoli is very, very tender and falling apart, 35–40 minutes. Check under the lid every now and again, and if the pot becomes too dry, add a bit more water.

Once the broccoli is very mushy, add the lemon juice and a bit of the zest along with the remaining ½ cup oil. Mash it all up with a hand masher until it gets an emulsified sheen and has the texture of baby food. Give it a taste and tweak the seasoning with more salt and/or lemon juice and zest to your liking.

Remove from the heat and serve warm or at room temperature atop toasted bread with your garnish of choice.

SOUP & SALAD TIME

Food does not need to be elaborate or complicated to be spectacular. Start with great ingredients and you get delicious results. It's as simple as that!

FULLY LOADED CHICKEN SOUP

- **SERVES 6–8**

For the dish that makes any home smell better, enter chicken soup. The chicken and the mirepoix serve as a soul-warming soup base for any nutrient-dense green or vegetable. Pea and sunflower shoots and petite broccoli florets are among some of the best end-of-soup add-ins. Stirring them in just before the soup comes off the heat makes their sweetness blossom in the broth. Fresh herbs and vegetables are the only suitable ones to use—never dried or frozen, as their flavor is a bit muddied. My preferred garnish right before serving is torn fresh dill and a nub of butter; together they take the comfort level of the soup over the top.

½ cup extra-virgin olive oil

3–4 tablespoons butter

2–3 medium yellow onions, finely chopped

1 fennel bulb, about 1 lb carrots, and/or 3–5 celery ribs, finely chopped

3 lb chicken, whole bird or bone-in, skin-on breasts

4 quarts water or good-quality unsalted chicken bone broth, or a combination

1–2 cups dry white wine

Kosher salt and freshly ground black pepper

Freshly grated nutmeg, for seasoning

1 lemon, halved

1–2 tablespoons runny honey

2–3 cups cooked rice and/or cooked broccoli florets or other vegetables (optional)

1 bunch fresh dill or flat-leaf parsley, big handful of pea shoots or fennel fronds, and/or other delicate greens of choice, roughly chopped

Grated Parmesan cheese, for serving

Butter-soaked toasted crusty bread, for serving

Place a Dutch oven or other large, heavy pot over medium heat. Add the oil, butter, onions, and fennel, carrots, and/or celery and sweat all the vegetables, stirring occasionally, until translucent, about 10 minutes. Add the chicken, water, and as much wine as you like and bring to a simmer. Adjust the heat to maintain a simmer and cook until the chicken is very tender, about 1 hour.

Transfer the chicken to a large platter, let cool just until it can be handled, and then pull the meat away from the bones, discarding the bones and skin. Pull or cut the meat into bite-size pieces and return it to the pot. Season the soup with salt and pepper, a few gratings of nutmeg, a squeeze or two of lemon juice, and honey to taste and return to a simmer.

If you like, add some cooked rice and or vegetables and then simmer the soup for a few minutes to heat through. Taste and adjust the seasonings with salt, pepper, nutmeg, lemon, and honey if needed.

Finish the soup in the final moments with copious amounts of herbs and/or shoots and a few twists of pepper. Serve piping hot with a dusting of Parmesan, and accompany with crusty bread.

SILKY VEGETABLE SOUP

- **SERVES 4–6**

This specific preparation is meant to be a pure expression of the main ingredient, highlighting clean and polished flavors you might not taste in its raw form. It is very simple, does not take long, and, if executed correctly, will blow your guests' minds. A high-powered blender and a fine-mesh sieve will be your best friends in achieving a soup of Michelin-star quality. Often, I like to use plain old water instead of stock to get the purest possible flavor of the star ingredient.

¾ cup (6 oz) butter

1 large sweet onion, diced

Kosher salt

4–5 lb stellar vegetable of choice, trimmed into nice, even pieces

Splash of dry white wine (optional)

Crème fraîche or heavy cream, for finishing (optional)

Fresh lemon juice or white wine vinegar, for finishing (optional)

Heat a large pot over medium heat. Add the butter and onion, toss in a pinch of salt, and sweat the onion, stirring occasionally, until translucent, about 6 minutes. Add the vegetable of choice and sweat for an additional 5–10 minutes.

Add the wine, if using, and deglaze the pot, stirring to dislodge any bits from the pot bottom, and then pour in enough water to nearly cover the vegetable. Bring to a simmer and simmer, stirring occasionally, just until the vegetable pieces are cooked through and not a moment more.

Remove from the heat and let cool slightly. Then, working in batches if necessary, transfer to a blender and purée until smooth. (A high-speed blender is best, but a regular blender will do; just be sure to run it long enough for a smooth result.) Pass the puréed soup through a fine-mesh sieve. (This step ensures the finest texture.) At this point, you can finish the soup with a bit of crème fraîche to give it an extra-luxurious mouthfeel.

The silky soup can be served hot or chilled. To serve hot, place in a heavy saucepan and heat gently to serving temperature. If serving chilled, transfer to an airtight container and refrigerate until cold. Taste and adjust the seasoning with salt if needed before serving. Also, check to see if a drop of lemon juice is needed to brighten the flavor. Then garnish with discretion, keeping in mind that the hot version will taste wildly different from the chilled and thus will be best suited to different garnishes.

ON SOUP

The making of a great soup, or even just a good one, is an art. Sometimes even trained professionals are unable to conjure up a preparation worthy of praise. Most do not control their creative urges and end up overcomplicating the ingredients list to no end. They recklessly pile on unnecessary garnishes, turning the soup into a shadow of what it once was. Others simply don't give a damn about soup at all!

The quality of a soup speaks directly to the talents of its maker and most certainly sets the tone for the dishes to follow. If you start a meal with a mucked-up soup, it's only going downhill from there.

The soup pot should never be treated as a garbage disposal, with the cook tossing in bits of this and that without a particular goal in mind. The soup will end up tasting vague and dull with bleak, muddy notes. There can, of course, be more than one star in the pot, like potato and leek or white bean and tomato. But the cook must always choose wisely and keep the number under control. When too many ingredients commingle in a pot, they inevitably cancel one another out, no matter how good their individual quality may be.

To alter or enhance the flavor profile of the main ingredient, I occasionally char it before adding it to the onion. This works particularly well with broccoli to get the boldest flavor, though it turns it a putrid color. Sometimes kissing the produce, like tomatoes or carrots, with billows of smoke from wood chips will bring out deeper, more sultry notes.

If the vegetables I am working with are of exceptional quality, then I want their pure taste to shine. Therefore, I will use water rather than stock to retain the pure taste. There are times, however, when stock has its place, as does deglazing the pot with wine or a spirit or adding bits of a salty pork product, such as bacon or guanciale. All of these additions can enhance and complement the soup.

When it comes to the garnish, the same mindset applies. We don't need an Eiffel Tower of embellishments. When you taste your final soup, think about what might be a nice enhancement rather than a distraction or, even worse, turn it into another dish entirely. Might a few batons of tart apple or a dollop of crème fraîche be all you need to make your parsnip soup pop? Will that sprinkle of chopped herbs or bacon kill your soup or lift it up to the heavens? I leave that decision entirely up to you. Whatever you choose, make sure to keep your creative impulses under control. If your soup turns out very good, exploding with its own true taste, it might very well need nothing more at all—though a drizzle of fine olive oil rarely ever hurts.

AN IMPRESSIVE POT OF BEANS

- ■ SERVES 4–6

Many people don't know that dried beans sitting on a pantry shelf have a life span. I am here to tell you that they do! A freshly dried bean gives an incomparable outcome compared to one that has kicked around the back of a cupboard for a couple of years. Interest in dried beans continues to rise, and now many farmers grow exceptional varieties that can be found at markets across the country and online. If you have come across freshly dried beans, soaking them for less time is much advised. You might not need to soak them at all, though some soaking makes them easier to digest. Once you have made a meal of the beans, the leftovers are perfection rolled into a chewy flour tortilla with melted cheese.

---

1 lb dried beans, such as Borlotti, pinto, or Alubia Blanca

1 cup extra-virgin olive oil, preferably a buttery one, plus more for finishing

1 sweet onion, diced small

Kosher salt

1–2 cups sherry

2 cloves garlic and/or bay leaves

Chopped fresh rosemary or thyme or toasted ground cumin or red chile flakes and fresh lemon juice, for finishing

In a bowl, combine the beans with water to cover and leave to soak overnight. The next day, drain them and then give them a good rinse.

Heat a Dutch oven or other large, heavy pot over medium heat. Add the oil and onion, toss in a couple of nice pinches of salt, and sweat the onion, stirring occasionally, until translucent, about 6 minutes.

Add the beans to the pot, then cover with an inch or so of water, pour in 1 cup of the sherry, and toss in the garlic and/or bay. Bring to a simmer, reduce the heat to medium-low, cover, and cook, stirring occasionally, until tender. (Every bean variety will have a different cooking time, and the times can vary from 45 minutes to 2 hours or longer. In general, the slower the beans cook, the better they'll be.) If the pot gets too dry, add a bit more water and sherry.

Once the beans are tender, season with more salt if needed. Rosemary can be a nice touch at the end, or you can finish with a pinch of cumin and a splash of lemon juice. I like to mash the beans slightly, adding a little extra water if needed, then emulsify it all with more oil, making a creamy mash. I always add an extra splash of sherry at the end for added punch. The beans should be very rich in olive oil and a bit boozy.

CHUNKY VEGETABLE SOUP WITH PISTOU

■ SERVES 6–8

This soup can dance with any season but always requires peak-season produce and common sense. In the springtime, flavors are best kept light and bright; fill the pot with green onions and garlic, sweet peas, petite turnips, fennel, and tender greens. By summer, the choices become bolder, with meaty nightshades like tomatoes, potatoes, and peppers along with chunks of zucchini and green beans. When early autumn arrives, it's time to showcase the last of the season's tomatoes, swirling them in alongside autumn squash and root-vegetable tops. Once the winter frost takes hold, only storage-type vegetables are left to mingle in the pot. Whatever vegetables you choose for the soup, be mindful to cook them well but not turn them to mush.

The herb or green in the pistou or pesto can be played with to fit the season as well, and the garlic in the sauce can be dialed up or down to provide more punch. Consider, too, offering bundles of soft fresh herbs as a great communal centerpiece for guests to pluck from and stir into their bowls. At a minimum, a hunk of Parmesan cheese and a grater, a nice olive oil, and a pepper mill should always be present for guests to dress their bowls. Serve with crusty bread or crostini.

---

1 cup dried beans, such as cannellini, navy, or cranberry

½ cup extra-virgin olive oil, plus more for serving

1 large onion, finely chopped

2–3 carrots, finely chopped

2–3 cloves garlic, thinly sliced

Kosher salt and freshly ground black pepper

Handful of plum tomatoes, peeled (optional)

1 cup dry white wine

4 cups water or vegetable broth, or as needed

2–3 lb peak-season vegetables (3 or 4 different types), trimmed and diced or sliced beautifully

3–4 fresh thyme sprigs

2 bay leaves

1 cup al dente cooked petite pasta, such as small shells or orzo (optional)

Spring Pistou (page 221) or seasonal pesto of choice

Wedge of Parmesan cheese, for serving

In a bowl, combine the beans with water to cover and leave to soak overnight. The next day, drain them, give them a good rinse, and transfer to a saucepan. Add water to cover generously, bring to a simmer over medium-high heat, adjust the heat to maintain a gentle simmer, and cook until tender, 1–2 hours, depending on the type of bean. Drain and set aside.

Place a Dutch oven or other large, heavy pot over medium heat. Add the oil, onion, carrots, garlic, and a hefty pinch of salt, and sweat the vegetables, stirring occasionally, until soft, about 8 minutes.

Add the tomatoes, if using, breaking them up a bit with your hands before dropping them into the pot, and then pour in the wine. Bring to a simmer and simmer for a few minutes. Then add the water, your beautiful seasonal vegetables, and the thyme and bay. Bring to a simmer, adjust the heat to maintain a steady simmer, and cook for about 20 minutes.

At this point, the vegetables should be nearly tender. Add the reserved beans and cook for 5–10 minutes to heat the beans through and finish cooking the vegetables.

Remove and discard the thyme and bay leaves. At the last minute, stir in the pasta, if using, and simmer just until heated. If the soup seems too thick, add more water or broth to thin as desired.

Serve the soup in wide bowls that proudly display the seasonal bounty. Finish each bowl with a heaping spoonful of the garlicky herbaceous pistou, then offer Parmesan and olive oil at the table.

GAZPACHO

■ SERVES 4–8

Although this famous ice-cold Spanish soup has countless variations, it should always be a piquant and refreshing contrast to the dog days of summer. The base of the soup, which traditionally includes fresh tomatoes, olive oil, and garlic, can be altered by incorporating everything from chiles and cucumbers to onions and herbs. I find that adding a bit of stone fruit, such as cherries, to the base imparts a beautiful depth of flavor and a subtle sweetness that help to distinguish the soup from a mere bowl of salsa.

The toppings can be a selection of vegetables that are already included in the soup base, like a fine dice of cucumber or halved cherry tomatoes, or brand new additions, such as torn olives, poached shrimp, or flowering herbs. Hard-boiled eggs and avocado are both wonderful garnishes and a good way to incorporate protein and rich fat. Simple additions like torn bread and croutons are nice too. On the hottest days, I've even floated broken-up ice as a garnish! Set lush bowls of finely manicured garnishes on the table for diners to add as they like.

As with nearly every recipe in this book, the success of this preparation depends on quality, balance, and contrast. Make sure to serve extra-crunchy bread alongside—the kind that has been liberally brushed with oil and then toasted until slightly burned. Pour a cold white wine that has a hint of sweetness to complement the bursts of heat from the chile.

About 1 cup pitted and chopped medium-ripe stone fruit, such as cherries or nectarines (optional)

2–3 medium-hot fresh red chiles, chopped

2 cucumbers, each about 4 inches long, peeled and chopped

2–3 lb tomatoes, peeled (see page 147)

3–4 cloves garlic, grated

1 cup extra-virgin olive oil, preferably a fruity and buttery one

Dash of sherry vinegar and/or runny honey

Kosher salt and freshly ground black pepper

Splash of ice water or handful of crushed ice, if needed

Selection of garnishes of choice (see headnote), for serving

Toasted bread (see headnote), for serving

In a food processor, combine the stone fruit (if using), chiles, and cucumbers and blitz until almost a purée. Add the tomatoes, garlic, and oil and blitz once again until the mixture is smooth. Add the vinegar and/or honey, season with salt and pepper, and pulse briefly to mix well. Taste and adjust the seasoning with salt, pepper, and vinegar and/or honey, then add the ice water to adjust the consistency if needed. Transfer to an airtight container and refrigerate until well chilled. At the same time, slip some bowls into the refrigerator to chill.

Just before serving, taste the soup one more time and adjust the seasoning as needed. (Chilling foods tempers their flavors and aromas.) Serve the soup extremely cold in well-chilled bowls that make you want to dig in. Set out a flurry of fun garnishes and a large side of toasted bread for guests to help themselves.

LITTLE GEMS ALMONDINE

■ SERVES 4–6

Little Gem lettuce has grown in popularity over the past few years, making an appearance—raw, marinated, grilled, and more—in nearly every posh restaurant on the map. But this small romaine type is not only popular among consumers but also growers. It is a fast-growing, consistent variety that yields the perfect personal-size lettuce. It can be cultivated year-round, is ideal for growing in compact spaces, and transplants with ease. Once the heads have reached their destined size, they bolt, shooting up a sign they are ready for the compost and no longer good for the plate.

4–8 heads Little Gem lettuce (1 or 2 heads per person, depending on size)

5 tablespoons butter

2–3 tablespoons extra-virgin olive oil

2 cloves garlic

Pinch of kosher salt

Pinch of smoked paprika (optional)

1–2 dashes aged sherry vinegar

½ cup slivered almonds, toasted

Torn fresh flat-leaf parsley leaves, for garnish

½ cup toasted bread crumbs

Maldon salt and freshly ground black pepper

Clean any unattractive outer leaves off the Little Gem heads. Trim the base of each head, then cut lengthwise into halves or quarters (depending on size), keeping each piece intact. Arrange cut side up on individual plates or a platter.

In a skillet, melt the butter with the olive oil over medium heat. Then, using a Microplane or other fine-rasp grater, grate the garlic directly into the pan. Add the kosher salt and paprika (if using) and cook until the mixture becomes obnoxiously aromatic—in the best way. Take a moment to inhale deeply and notice what pleasure these fragrances deliver!

Add the vinegar, give the mixture a taste, think what it might need, and adjust. The flavor should be rich, bright, and well seasoned to balance the high water content of the greens.

Moments before you are ready to serve, and not a moment sooner, spoon the warm dressing over the Little Gems and garnish with a storm of almonds, parsley, and bread crumbs. Finish with Maldon salt and several twists of pepper and serve.

SHAVED CELERY SALAD
WITH GRAPES, PISTACHIOS, MINT & FETA

- SERVES 4–6

The flavor difference between farm-grown celery and agribusiness celery is dramatic. Upon first bite of a farm-cultivated rib, you'll understand the true punch celery can bring when it hasn't been saturated with water. The yield proves to be much higher as well, as the heads seldom have damaged outer ribs that must be plucked off. Reserved no longer just for flavoring stocks and stews, celery now shines in a marinade, pickled, or sautéed in butter and wine. It is also perfectly suited for a raw shaved salad. The young leaves can be used as a garnish, just as you would use an herb.

2–3 cups thinly sliced celery, cut on the diagonal

1–2 cups green grapes, halved

Kosher salt and freshly ground black pepper

Extra-virgin olive oil, for drizzling

1 lemon, halved

1 cup shelled pistachios, toasted and roughly chopped

Handful of mild fresh mint leaves

²/₃ cup crumbled sheep's milk feta cheese

In a bowl, combine the celery and grapes. Season with salt and drizzle with just enough oil to coat lightly. Toss gently, add a nice squeeze of lemon, and toss again. Add the pistachios and mint, mix again, and taste. Adjust with oil, lemon, and salt as needed.

Arrange on a serving plate and top with the cheese, a few twists of pepper, and a fine drizzle of oil. Serve right away.

ON SALAD

Some say that the true test of a cook's talent is a simple soup. Others might say it's a scrambled egg or an omelet. I say that cooks are only as good as the simplest of green salads they can make, but I'm weird like that.

Salads can contain a whole mess of vegetables, from raw to cooked. The composed ones you'll find in this chapter share some common qualities: a fresh, airy texture, a fatty yet tart taste, and delicately applied dressing. Nearly any combination of ingredients will work in a salad as long as you create a smart mixture and you have the fundamentals—fat, acid, salt—on hand. Creating a "smart" mixture means not combining the softest of lettuces, such as microgreens or buttery mâche, with tougher varieties, like kale or mustards. One won't do anything to benefit the other. Salads should ebb and flow with the seasons. That means the lettuce choices and any additions should be complementary expressions of what is available at that time of year.

While much thought and planning can go into making a composed salad, the only things you need to make the very best of salads, beyond stellar greens, are a premium oil, a sting of acid, and a bit of salt. When these things are added in harmony, the salad will go from bleak to exquisite, and you'll know by its taste that you've nailed it.

Although this all may sound basic and simple, making a salad is actually one of the most difficult things to do well. You need to be in tune with the ingredients you are adding—the perfect sprinkle of salt, the right amount of acid, and the nicest, gentlest drizzle of oil—to enhance the goodies in the bowl while not weighing them down. When used in just the right amount, these elements coax the flavors out of the greens, rather than leaving them naked or soggy.

The greens and/or vegetables should be cleaned well in very, very cold water to make them extra perky and then thoroughly dried. No one likes a gritty, soggy salad! Place the clean and well-dried greens in an oversize mixing bowl to allow ample room for the greens to dance around your fingers.

When it comes to dressing a salad, you'll usually want to do it at the very last minute so the greens don't wilt. Also, go light at first, because once a salad is overdressed, you can never go back.

Taste at every step of the way and always with a discerning palate. Try the greens alone and then try a few nibbles with all the components. This is how to see if you're on the right track. When it tastes of perfection, you'll know.

SWISS CHARD CHIFFONADE
WITH LEMON, PINE NUTS, BASIL & BREAD CRUMBS

■ SERVES 4–6

Commonly served either marinated or sautéed, Swiss chard is rarely served raw but it happens to be one of our favorite ways to enjoy it. A member of the beet family, it becomes tender with earthy sweetness once our weather begins to cool in the fall, making it ideal for using in a salad. We think it just might be the new kale. This salad is wonderful alone but becomes a whole new dish when spooned over pesto-dressed orzo pasta or risotto that has been tossed with butter and Parmesan.

Be sure to select young, tender leaves for this recipe. After removing the stems, do not discard them! Chop them up and make a quick pickle to serve with pâté, stir them into chicken soup (page 96), or sauté them with a bit of garlic for a crunchy accompaniment to steamed fish.

2–3 bunches young, tender Swiss chard, stems removed

Nice amount of torn fresh basil and flat-leaf parsley leaves

About 1½ cups bread crumbs

1 cup pine nuts, toasted

Extra-virgin olive oil, for dressing

Kosher salt and freshly ground black pepper

Grated zest and juice of 2 lemons

Parmesan cheese, for garnish (optional)

Working in batches, stack the leaves and then fold them over on themselves lengthwise. Using a very sharp knife, cut crosswise into strips no more than ½ inch wide.

Scoop the ribbons into a generous serving bowl and add most of the herbs, bread crumbs, and pine nuts, setting aside some of each for topping. Drizzle on some oil, coating lightly, and sprinkle with salt. Toss lightly, then add the lemon juice and a bit of zest and a few grinds of pepper and toss again. Taste and adjust with more oil and lemon as needed, then season well with salt and pepper.

Top with the reserved herbs, bread crumbs, and pine nuts and garnish with Parmesan cheese, if using. Serve right away.

HARVEST TIP

Swiss chard has a compound seed structure, which means there are multiple shoots within a single seed. Once the seeds are planted, you will need to thin the seedlings when they are about 4 inches tall to achieve a lush growth. When the leafy stalks grow to about a foot tall, harvest only the outer leaves to keep continuous growth in the center of the plant for weeks to come.

ANCHOVY VINAIGRETTE

Makes about ¾ cup

4–6 anchovy fillets in oil
1 clove garlic
Kosher salt and freshly ground black pepper
1 teaspoon Dijon mustard
2 tablespoons red wine vinegar
Squeeze of fresh lemon juice
1 large egg yolk (freshest you can find!)
½ cup extra-virgin olive oil

This is superb made with a mortar and pestle, but it can also be made with a whisk or thrown together in a food processor or blender. In a small bowl, combine the anchovies, garlic, and a pinch of salt and mash together with a fork to a paste. Mix in the mustard, vinegar, and lemon juice followed by the egg yolk. Then slowly stream in the oil while mixing constantly until you have a shiny, fully emulsified vinaigrette. Season with salt and pepper.

Always make this vinaigrette right before you're ready to dress the salad. It does not age well in the refrigerator.

SHALLOT VINAIGRETTE

Makes about 1½ cups

3 shallots, minced
⅓ cup moscatel vinegar or rice vinegar
Pinch of sugar
Kosher salt and freshly ground black pepper
About 1 cup extra-virgin olive oil

In a small bowl, stir together the shallots, vinegar, sugar, and a pinch of salt. Let sit to macerate for at least 30 minutes or even for a day or two. Whisk in the oil and season with more salt and with pepper.

The vinaigrette will keep in an airtight container in the refrigerator for up to a week or so, but the flavors lose their brightness the longer the vinaigrette sits, so it is best to use it within the first couple of days.

SHERRY & EGG VINAIGRETTE

Makes about 1½ cups

1 large egg yolk
½ cup grapeseed oil
½ cup extra-virgin olive oil
3 tablespoons aged sherry vinegar
Dash of Worcestershire sauce (optional)
Dash of Tabasco sauce (optional)
Kosher salt and freshly ground black pepper

In a bowl, using a whisk or fork, whisk together vigorously the egg yolk, grapeseed oil, olive oil, vinegar, and the Worcestershire and Tabasco sauces, if using, until creamy and emulsified. If the vinaigrette is too thick, whisk in a splash of water to thin to a good consistency. (You can also whip up this dressing in a blender or small food processor.) Whisk in a hefty pinch of salt and several twists of pepper, then taste and adjust the seasoning if needed. Use right away (enjoy it on a simple leafy green salad), or store in an airtight container in the refrigerator up to about 1 week.

EXTRA-CRUNCHY GARLICKY BREAD CRUMBS

Makes about 1 cup

1 cup panko or unseasoned coarse bread crumbs
⅓ cup extra-virgin olive oil
2 teaspoons kosher salt
1 clove garlic, smashed
Suggested add-ins: freshly ground black pepper, red chile flakes or cayenne pepper, grated Parmesan cheese, and/or herbs (such as oregano, thyme, or rosemary) and spices of choice

In a sauté pan over medium heat, warm the oil and garlic, stirring occasionally, until the garlic is fragrant, about 2 minutes. Add the bread crumbs and stir to toast until evenly golden brown, 2–3 minutes.

Remove from the heat and remove and discard the browned garlic pieces if you like. Toss in any of the suggested add-ins that appeal or any other seasoning you think might be nice. Enjoy with everything and on anything!

ESCAROLE
WITH RED ONION, HAZELNUTS & YOUNG PECORINO

- SERVES 4–6

Escarole is one of the more standardized and one of the most versatile members of the chicory family. Most escarole seeds found nowadays are the self-blanching type, which require less work to achieve tender, palatable leaves. Escarole is best grown in the shoulder seasons of spring and fall, as extreme heat causes bitter, unpleasant flavor. Whether used in a salad, soup, or stew, the younger, smaller heads are always the best ones to choose. With one bite, you will know if your escarole is past its prime or ready for primetime.

1–2 small-to-medium heads escarole

½ cup thinly shaved red onion or shallot, soaked in ice water for about 10 minutes

⅓ cup extra-virgin olive oil

¾ cup peeled hazelnuts, toasted and roughly chopped

Kosher salt and freshly ground black pepper

1 cup grated buttery, semifirm cheese, such as a young pecorino or toma

Juice of 1–2 lemons

Trim the escarole head(s), then cut into bite-size pieces. Transfer to a large bowl. Drain the onion and give it a gentle squeeze to remove excess water. (Soaking the onion in ice water gives it superb crunch and mellows its sharp flavor.) Add the onion to the bowl with the greens.

Drizzle in the oil and add the nuts and a big pinch of salt. Give everything a light toss and then add the cheese, some lemon juice, and a few cracks of pepper. Toss everything again and give the salad a taste. Adjust with more oil, lemon juice, salt, and pepper if needed.

Once you are satisfied with the flavors, plate the salad high and proud on individual plates and top with the goodies left at the bottom of the bowl. Serve right away.

PETITE KALE & MUSTARD GREENS
WITH FALL SQUASH, SMOKED GOUDA & TOASTED PECAN DRESSING

■ SERVES 4–6

Is there ever a present moment in farming? In August our greenhouse is seeded full of winter produce, much of which won't be ready to harvest until late November and some, like leeks, won't come out until May! Though slow growing, the kale and mustard greens we plant are much more tender than those we grow outside in the warmer months. Their sugars creep out due to the cold, humid environment, and their leaves stay soft, free of scalding sun rays.

FOR THE DRESSING

¾ cup pecans, toasted until golden and fragrant

½ cup walnut or hazelnut oil, or grapeseed oil cut with extra-virgin olive oil

⅓ cup cider vinegar

⅓ cup water

¼ cup dark maple syrup

1–2 teaspoons Dijon mustard

1 tiny clove garlic

Pinch of cayenne pepper

1 small shallot, minced

Kosher salt and freshly ground black pepper

—

2 lb fall squash such as delicata, red kuri, or candy roaster, plus a peeled hunk for shaving

Extra-virgin olive oil, for coating the squash

Kosher salt and freshly ground black pepper

1 cup pecan halves

1 lb baby kale and mustard greens, large ribs removed and torn

1 shallot, thinly sliced

4 oz smoked Gouda cheese, shredded

1 lemon, halved

Several torn fresh flat-leaf parsley leaves, for garnish

To make the dressing, in a blender, combine the pecans, walnut oil, vinegar, water, maple syrup, mustard, garlic, and cayenne and blend until perfectly smooth. Transfer to a bowl, stir in the shallot, and season with salt and black pepper. Set aside.

Preheat the oven to 400°F. Peel and seed the squash, then cut into 1-inch cubes. Transfer the cubes to a sheet pan, drizzle with oil, sprinkle liberally with salt, and toss until well coated. Spread the cubes in a single layer. Roast until caramelized and tender when pierced with a knife tip, 25–35 minutes. Remove from the oven and let cool.

Reduce the oven temperature to 350°F. Spread the pecans on a small sheet pan, place in the oven, and toast, stirring once or twice, until golden brown and aromatic, 7–10 minutes. Pour onto a plate and let cool.

In a large bowl, combine the mixed greens, cooled squash, shallot, and most of the Gouda and pecans, reserving some of both for garnish. Using a vegetable peeler, shave the hunk of raw squash into ribbons directly into the bowl. Drizzle ½ cup of the dressing over the top, add a squeeze of lemon, and mix by hand just until lightly and evenly coated. (Store any extra dressing in the refrigerator for up to 1 week.) Adjust with lemon, salt, and pepper for more punch and then garnish with the reserved cheese and nuts. Tuck in the torn parsley and serve right away.

FALL RADISH SALAD
WITH WALNUTS, SESAME & MINT

■ SERVES 4–6

As fall commences, the chilly evening air does magical things to root vegetables like radishes. Their tops begin to weaken and their energy shifts to their roots to form sugar, which they use for survival. Their usual spicy flavor begins to mellow, developing a fruit-like sweetness, and they take on a nice crunch.

4–8 medium-to-large assorted fall radishes, such as watermelon, green luobo, and Spanish black

1 cup or so walnut halves, toasted and lightly crushed

½ cup toasted sesame seeds, plus more for garnish

½ cup buttery extra-virgin olive oil

Juice of 1 large lemon

Maldon salt and freshly ground black pepper

Handful of fresh mint leaves

Handful of fresh flat-leaf parsley leaves

Runny honey, for drizzling

HOT TIP To give extra crunch to any root vegetable or onion, give them a plunge in ice water after you've sliced them. A prolonged soak will also help to mellow the flavor.

Using a vegetable peeler, remove any blemishes or tough skin from the radishes. Using a mandoline or a sharp knife, cut the radishes into slices about the thickness of a quarter. Cut the slices into half-moons or whatever shape is bite-size and would be pleasantly received.

In a bowl, combine the radishes, walnuts, sesame seeds, oil, and lemon juice, season liberally with salt, and toss to mix well. Tear some of the mint and parsley leaves, leaving the rest whole, and add them all to the bowl. Massage everything together with your hands, then taste for seasoning and adjust as needed.

Garnish with a drizzle of honey, a dusting of pepper, and a sprinkle of sesame seeds and serve.

FATTY BISTRO SALAD

■ SERVES 4–6

This salad is meant to be as piquant and tangy as it is rich and fatty. Batavia lettuce varieties are the best choice here. Available in an array of colors, they are a head lettuce but with loose, frilly leaves and a little more tooth than butter lettuce. The heads have a dense core, and the leaves have enough body to stand up to an emulsified dressing and rich strands of Gruyère cheese. Make sure to use plenty of cheese and black pepper, to pile the salad high, and to dress it with care. Pair with a floral white or light red wine and with a crisp baguette and cold butter.

FOR THE DRESSING

1 cup grapeseed oil

⅓ cup red wine vinegar

3 tablespoons Dijon mustard

Kosher salt and freshly ground black pepper

—

1–2 heads frilly red leaf and/or green leaf lettuce

6–8 petite radishes, thinly shaved and immersed in ice water

4–6 oz Gruyère cheese, grated on the medium holes of a box grater

1 shallot, thinly shaved

1–2 handfuls of herb croutons

Kosher salt and freshly ground black pepper

To make the dressing, in a blender, combine the oil, vinegar, mustard, 2 pinches of salt, and several cracks of pepper and blend until smooth and emulsified. It should have a creamy and shiny appearance and the consistency of thick heavy cream. Thin with a little water if needed. Give it a taste and adjust if needed. It should be quite pungent, salty, and Dijon-forward. Set aside.

Trim the lettuce head(s) and tear the leaves into manageable pieces. Place in a large bowl. Drain the radishes, pat dry, and add to the lettuce along with half of the Gruyère, the shallot, and the croutons. Drizzle the dressing over the top and mix lovingly by hand. Season with salt and plenty of pepper and mix again.

Plate up nice and high, using two hands, and finish the airy mound with the remaining Gruyère followed by more cracked pepper. Serve right away.

CHICORIES
WITH ANCHOVY, NUT CRUMBS & BLUE CHEESE–SHERRY VINAIGRETTE

■ SERVES 4–6

Chicories and lettuces belong to the same botanical family, but chicories tend to be heartier and have a more assertive flavor. Their bitter notes are perfectly complemented by richer, fattier dressings and salty, sweet bits. For this salad, we love to use tender heads of Belgian endive for their sturdy texture and delicate flavor, though a mixture of chicories, such as radicchio (Treviso or Chioggia) and frisée, would also be suitable.

FOR THE VINAIGRETTE

3–4 oz blue cheese, such as Roquefort

½ cup extra-virgin olive oil

¼ cup full-fat buttermilk or crème fraîche

2 tablespoons sherry vinegar

1 tablespoon Dijon mustard

1 drop agave nectar

Kosher salt

Fresh lemon juice, for thinning (optional)

—

1 cup nuts of choice

½ cup toasted bread crumbs

Splash of extra-virgin olive oil

Kosher salt

1 lb assorted chicories, such as Belgian endive, radicchio, and frisée

Maldon salt and freshly ground black pepper

3–5 anchovy fillets in olive oil, torn into ½-inch bits

Chopped chives or fresh flat-leaf parsley leaves, for garnish

To make the vinaigrette, in a food processor, combine the cheese, oil, buttermilk, vinegar, mustard, agave nectar, and a pinch of kosher salt and pulse until moderately smooth. Adjust the consistency with a bit of lemon juice or water if needed, then taste and adjust with salt if needed. Set aside.

Preheat the oven to 350°F. Spread the nuts on a small sheet pan, place in the oven, and toast, stirring once or twice, until golden brown and aromatic, 7–10 minutes. Pour onto a plate and let cool. Transfer to the food processor and pulse to a crumb-like consistency. Add the bread crumbs, oil, and a pinch of kosher salt and pulse a few times. The mixture should be sandy, rich, and nicely seasoned. Adjust with more oil and salt if needed.

Trim the chicories and cut them into shapes that are neither too big nor too small, being careful not to bruise them. For a salad course, you will want 1–2 cups cut-up greens per person. Transfer the chicories to a large bowl.

Dress the chicories with the vinaigrette, coating them lightly. You may not need all the vinaigrette; store the remainder in an airtight container in the refrigerator for up to 1 week. Season with Maldon salt and pepper.

Arrange the dressed chicories on a platter or individual plates and disperse the anchovy bits evenly throughout, tucking them into pockets and crevices so they don't fall off the leaves. Scatter the walnut mixture over the top and garnish with bursts chives or parsley and pepper. Serve right away.

HOT TIP Grapes make a lovely addition to this salad. Boldly flavored varieties, like Concord or Thomcat, can be sourced from many farmers' markets in late summer or early fall.

FRIENDS & FAMILY

We're not here for a long time, we're here for a good time. Huzzah!

BLANCHED LEEKS WITH TOMA & HAZELNUTS

■ SERVES 4–6

Leeks are much easier to grow than onions in a home garden. They are spatially efficient and can be deliciously useful at any size. They are also slightly less time-consuming to plant than their onion relatives. Baby leek shoots are stuck deep into a hole, with a couple of inches of their green tops poking out, so they develop an extra-long, tender white base. They can grow into early winter and are hardy enough to withstand frosty ground. Although you may have tossed the tougher darker green tops in the past, stop as of now! They simply require more cooking or blanching than the tender white bases. You can use them as wraps for tiny edible parcels, and when chopped up after a good blanching, they are sublime tossed into an omelet or quiche.

FOR THE LEEKS

Kosher salt and freshly ground black pepper

6–10 baby leeks, or
4–6 medium leeks

½ cup hazelnuts, toasted and peeled

¼ lb toma or Parmesan cheese

Extra-virgin oil, for drizzling

FOR THE VINAIGRETTE

2 tablespoons sherry, Cabernet, or moscatel vinegar

1–2 tablespoons Dijon mustard

1 shallot, finely chopped

½ cup extra-virgin olive oil, walnut oil, or hazelnut oil

Small handful of chopped fresh flat-leaf parsley leaves

To prepare the leeks, bring a large pot of water to a simmer and add about 1 teaspoon salt.

While the water is heating, cut off the dark green tops of the leeks and reserve for another use. Cut the tender white bottoms in half lengthwise. Rinse the leeks free of dirt and debris by fanning the layers under a cold stream of water. Trim off the bottom hairs right to the root, keeping the layers together, and discard any damaged outer layers.

Cut the leek halves in half lengthwise. Trim the tops as needed to keep all the pieces roughly the same length. Divide the leeks into even bundles and tie each bundle with kitchen twine to keep it together.

Place the bundles into the salted simmering water and cook until the leeks are nearly fork-tender, about 15 minutes. The cooking time will depend on the size of the leeks, so adjust the time accordingly.

Remove the bundles from the water and snip the twine to release the excess water and steam. Let the leeks cool to room temperature.

While the leeks are cooling, make the vinaigrette. In a small bowl, whisk together the vinegar, mustard, and shallot with a fork. Then slowly add the oil, whisking constantly until emulsified. Stir in the parsley and set aside.

Cut the cooled leeks into ½–¾-inch pieces. Transfer the leeks to a bowl, add the vinaigrette, and toss to coat well. Season with salt and pepper, toss again, and let sit for 10 minutes.

Arrange the leeks in a thin layer on a serving plate. (I like to arrange them in a ring mold to keep a clean shape.) Top the leeks with the hazelnuts and then, using a Microplane ribbon grater or the large holes of a box grater, shower with ribbons of toma until the leeks are barely visible. Finish with a drizzle of olive oil and a dusting of pepper and serve.

A PHENOMENAL POTATO PURÉE & MASHED POTATO SANDWICH

■ SERVES 4–6

Butter makes or breaks mashed potatoes, and this style of mashed potato does not go light on the butter. These potatoes turn out silky smooth and take a little more time and care than most simple mashes, but they are truly phenomenal. According to my Irish grandmother, when you have leftover mashed potatoes, you should always make a kick-ass mashed-potato sandwich the next day.

2 lb waxy new potatoes, unpeeled

Kosher salt

1 lb (2 sticks) cold butter, cubed

2–3 cups whole milk, warmed

Kosher salt

Pinch of freshly ground white pepper

FOR THE DAY-AFTER SANDWICH

Grab 2 slices of enriched white bread and liberally butter each slice on both sides. Top a slice with mashed potatoes, making the layer about 1½ inches thick. Sprinkle the potatoes with kosher salt and freshly ground black pepper and then close the sandwich. Heat a nonstick skillet over low heat, add the sandwich, and cook low and slow, turning once, until golden brown on both sides and barely warm through-out. It must not be too hot. Serve with a side of gravy or jam. It's a fine thing!

In a large, heavy saucepan, combine the potatoes with water to cover generously, then toss in a few courageous pinches of salt. Bring to a simmer over medium heat and cook until tender, about 20 minutes. The timing depends on the size of the potatoes. They are ready if when you stab a potato about two-thirds of the way through with a thin, sharp knife and then lift it, it falls from the knife.

Drain the potatoes, let cool until they can be handled, and then peel them with your hands and a paring knife. Fit a food mill with the finest disc, then pass the potatoes through the mill back into the pan.

Place the pan with the potatoes over very low heat to remove any excess moisture, stirring continuously so they do not burn. Then toss in a handful of the butter cubes, follow with a ladle of milk, and then whisk until the dairy is absorbed. Repeat with another handful of butter cubes and a little more milk, again whisking until absorbed. Repeat until all the butter has been incorporated, then whisk in a little more milk if needed to achieve a luscious consistency.

Season the velvety potato purée with salt and white pepper and serve warm.

MY GRANDPA'S ONIONS

From casual summer dinners to cowboy-centric gatherings in California, these onions have made an appearance at nearly every family barbecue my entire life. They are easy, impressive, beautifully sweet, and, some even say, succulent.

Be very generous when adding lumps of cold butter to these onions. It is not the time to be bashful, and all that creamy butter will indeed take them to a whole new level. They are a perfect accompaniment to grilled beef on a late-summer eve and are even better the next day on a sandwich with the leftover beef bits and horseradish.

Prepare a grill for direct cooking over medium heat. Place a couple (or more) of unpeeled, medium-size red onions on the grill grate and cook them the same way you would cook a potato in the oven, for about 1 hour, rotating them every so often.

Once the onions are tender throughout, take them inside, trim off their ends, and remove their skins like a jacket. The onion inside will be tender and full of sweetness and flavor. Put them into a bowl and, holding with tongs and using a knife, chop them into roughly 2-inch pieces. Toss them while hot with plenty of cold butter, some kosher salt, and a dusting of freshly ground black pepper.

These onions are also very fine served slightly chilled as an hors d'oeuvre or picnic accompaniment, with a little extra-virgin olive oil drizzled over the top.

TARTE FLAMBÉE

■ SERVES 3–4

A tarte flambée conjures the notion of pizza but is much lighter, with a cracker-like crust. It is perfect for warm summer evenings when you are craving pizza but also can't quite stomach something that heavy. The dough is easy to make, and the ingredients for it are on hand in most kitchens. The topping, which can be tweaked for the season, is a great way to use up random bits and bobs you have floating around in your refrigerator. The sauce can be cream-based like béchamel or a seasoned crème fraîche, a red sauce made from tomato or pepper purée, or even a green sauce. For cheese, low-moisture mozzarella and Parmesan work well, as do crumbles of a soft cheese, such as Boursin or chèvre, or a good melting cheese, like Gruyère or Comté. Top the cheese with any random bits you have floating around in your refrigerator—shaved vegetables, caramelized onions, or thinly sliced mushrooms or charcuterie. Any combination you choose will be fabulous.

FOR THE DOUGH

1 cup all-purpose flour, plus more for dusting

1½ teaspoons baking powder

½ teaspoon kosher salt

2 teaspoons extra-virgin olive oil

1 large egg yolk

——

Sauce, cheese, and topping of choice (see headnote)

Torn fresh herbs of choice, grated cheese, and freshly ground black pepper, for garnish

To make the dough, place a pizza stone or steel, a large cookie sheet (rimless sheet pan), or a large sheet pan on the middle rack of the oven and preheat the oven to 450°F for at least 30 minutes.

In a medium bowl, whisk together the flour, baking powder, and salt. In a small bowl, whisk together the oil and egg yolk until blended. Then add the oil mixture to the flour mixture and mix together until a shaggy dough forms.

Lightly dust a work surface with flour, then dump the dough out onto it. Knead the dough until it is smooth and elastic, 2–3 minutes. Cover with a kitchen towel and let rest for a few minutes.

Clean the work surface and dust again lightly with flour. Divide the dough into 2 or 3 pieces. Place a piece on the floured surface and roll out into a thin round or oval. Line a cookie sheet (or overturned sheet pan) with parchment paper and transfer the dough to the parchment. Repeat with the remaining dough and transfer to the parchment.

Top the dough with the sauce, cheese, and topping of choice. Be careful not to overload the crusts or the tarts will not cook properly.

Slide the parchment with the tarts directly onto the stone or pan in the oven. Bake until the crust is golden and crispy and the top is browned and melty, 15–20 minutes. Carefully remove from the oven, garnish with herbs, a dusting of cheese, and a few grinds of pepper, and serve warm.

LEMONY BEETS WITH TOASTED BUCKWHEAT GROATS, MARJORAM & STRACCIATELLA

■ SERVES 4–6

Beets are often displayed with their vitamin-rich tops still attached, but when stored together, the greens and the root age at very different rates. After a couple of days, the tops begin to lose their luster, while the roots will keep for weeks. Always trim off the tops immediately upon arriving home and cook them soon after in a soup or sauté. The roots can be peeled and shaved raw, pickled, boiled, or roasted. For this salad, you can either boil or roast the beets with their skins on, then remove the skins by rubbing them off with a towel while the beets are still quite warm. Heat is your friend here and will make this somewhat difficult task quite easy. If you can't even fathom the thought of red-bleeding beets covering your hands—and your kitchen—use golden beets, which leave much less of a mark but are equally delicious.

---

12 or so small beets, depending on size, greens removed

¾ cup buckwheat groats

Kosher salt

Grated zest and juice of 2–3 lemons

About ½ cup extra-virgin olive oil

Handful of torn fresh marjoram leaves, plus more for garnish

1–2 tablespoons thinly sliced shallot

½–1 teaspoon finely chopped Fresno or other fresh green chile, or pinch of red chile flakes (optional)

½ lb stracciatella or burrata cheese

1 cup or so baby arugula

Flavored extra-virgin olive oil, such as Agrumato tangerine olive oil, for finishing

Maldon salt and freshly ground black pepper

To boil the beets, place them in a large saucepan, add water to cover, and bring to a boil over high heat. Reduce the heat to a simmer and simmer until tender when pierced with a knife, 20–40 minutes, depending on size. To roast them, preheat the oven to 400°F. Arrange the beets in a single layer in a baking pan and roast until tender when pierced with a knife, 30–45 minutes, depending on size.

While the beets are cooking, toast the buckwheat groats. In a dry skillet, toast the groats over medium heat, stirring often, until they begin to exude a nutty aroma and turn deep gold, about 2 minutes. Pour into a small bowl and set aside.

Once the beets are cool enough to handle, rub the skins off with paper towels or use a kitchen towel you don't mind staining. Cut them into bite-size pieces and let cool. Place in a bowl and dress with kosher salt, a bit of lemon zest, ample lemon juice, and the olive oil, adjusting the amounts to suit your taste. Add the marjoram, shallot, and chile (if using) and stir gently to mix well.

Divide the beets among individual bowls and top with dollops of the stracciatella, dividing it evenly. Sprinkle the toasted groats over the top and make each serving extra pretty with more marjoram and the peppery arugula. Finish with a drizzle of flavored olive oil and a dusting of Maldon salt and pepper and serve.

GRILLED ZUCCHINI WITH NUT SALSA, MINT & RICOTTA

■ **SERVES 4**

The key to avoiding a soggy mess when grilling summer squash is not to cut them too small and to make sure the fire is very, very hot. Also, it is not wise to season the pieces with salt in advance, as salt draws out moisture, leaving the outside of each piece wet, which prevents a good sear. We do not like to cook the life out of any vegetable, so we don't let the zucchini spend more than a few moments over the heat. For recipes like this one where squash is the star, we always look for petite ones. They will inevitably have more flavor, less water, and a lower seed content. Larger squash are best turned into a soup or quick bread. If you come across squash blossoms, make sure they are free of bugs and debris, then snip them with scissors over the top of the finished dish for an eye-catching garnish.

FOR THE SALSA

1 cup nuts, such as walnuts, peeled hazelnuts, or almonds

½ cup extra-virgin olive oil

2 tablespoons white wine vinegar

3–6 anchovy fillets in olive oil

1–2 cloves garlic, grated

Grated zest and juice of 1 lemon

Light drizzle of runny honey

Kosher salt and freshly ground black pepper

—

2–3 lb small zucchini, such as Costata Romanesco, cut lengthwise into batons

Extra-virgin olive oil, for drizzling

Kosher salt and freshly ground black pepper

2–3 cloves garlic, sliced

Handfuls of fresh mint, basil, and flat-leaf parsley leaves, torn

1–2 cups whole-milk ricotta cheese

Dash of heavy cream

Maldon salt, for finishing

Vincotto (see page 180), for finishing

Grilled ciabatta, for serving

To make the salsa, preheat the oven to 350°F. Spread the nuts on a small sheet pan, place in the oven, and toast, stirring once or twice, until golden brown and aromatic, 7–10 minutes. Pour onto a plate and let cool.

Transfer the nuts to a food processor. Add the oil, vinegar, anchovies, garlic, a little zest and a few drops of juice from the lemon, the honey, a few pinches of kosher salt, and several twists of pepper and pulse until a coarse paste forms, thinning it with more acid and/or oil as needed. Give it a taste and adjust as needed. It should be quite bold in flavor, with aggressively garlicky, nutty, and salty notes. Set aside.

Prepare a grill for direct-heat cooking over high heat. The grill must be raging hot so the squash will sear quickly.

Lay the zucchini batons on a sheet pan or in a shallow bowl and drizzle with oil. Once the grill is hot—and not a moment before—sprinkle the zucchini with salt and arrange it on the grill grate. Grill until nicely seared with a bit of char on all sides and just slightly tender. Don't move the batons as they are searing and be careful not to overcook the squash or it will turn to mush.

While the zucchini is cooking, scatter the garlic in the sheet pan or bowl. Once the zucchini is done, transfer it to the pan or bowl, drizzle with a little oil, season with pepper, and toss gently to mix. Sprinkle some torn herb leaves onto the warm squash and mix again to perfume.

To serve, spoon the ricotta into a small bowl and whip with the cream until very creamy. Arrange the ricotta on a serving platter or individual plates in some casual schmears. Lay the zucchini batons on top and drizzle the nut salsa over the zucchini. Sprinkle with Maldon salt and more herbs and finish with a drizzle of vincotto. Serve with the bread alongside.

CREAMY KALE & LEEKS WITH PISTACHIOS

■ SERVES 4

As proven true with the classic creamed spinach, the healthiest of greens can become the most indulgent dish when paired with silky cream and aromatics. Dial up the amount of cream and toss it all with chewy pasta, a knob of butter, and loads of freshly grated Parm on a chilly winter night.

4 tablespoons butter

1–2 tablespoons extra-virgin olive oil

2–4 medium leeks, depending on size, white part only, sliced

1 sweet onion, julienned or diced

1–2 cloves garlic, thinly sliced

Kosher salt and freshly ground black pepper

Pinch of red chile flakes (optional)

1 cup heavy cream

1 teaspoon Dijon mustard

Grated zest and juice of 1 lemon

Freshly grated nutmeg, for seasoning

2 lb Tuscan (lacinato) kale, stems and ribs removed and leaves chopped or sliced into ribbons

¾ cup unsalted pistachios, toasted and finely chopped

Grated Parmesan cheese, for garnish

Toasted bread crumbs for garnish

Torn or chopped fresh flat-leaf parsley and/or thyme leaves, for garnish

Place a pan large enough to accommodate all the kale over medium heat. Add the butter, oil, leeks, onion, garlic, a few generous pinches of salt, and the chile flakes (if using) and sweat the vegetables, stirring occasionally, until the onion and leeks are translucent, 5–7 minutes. Add the cream, mustard, a bit of the lemon zest, and a dusting of nutmeg, stir well, and bring to the gentlest of simmers, stirring from time to time.

Add some of the kale in a single layer, toss in a splash of water (or broth if you prefer), cover the pan, and let the kale wilt. Repeat with the remaining kale, adding a layer at a time, until all the kale is in the pan. Do not add more water unless the cream has reduced significantly.

Continue to cook the kale over medium heat until it is very dark green and has a creamy consistency, 5–7 minutes. Then toss in the buttery pistachios, leaving behind a small handful for the garnish. Check for seasoning and adjust the brightness with lemon zest and juice as needed, then finish with several twists of pepper.

Transfer to a serving dish and top with a shower of Parmesan, bread crumbs, parsley, and the reserved pistachios. Serve at once.

WHOLE ROASTED EGGPLANT WITH BACON & HAZELNUTS

■ SERVES 6–8

Brimming with Mediterranean flavors—salty pork, orange, garlic, and nuts—this dish works best with petite globe eggplant varieties, like Rosita. Their not-too-big and not-too-tiny size aligns well with the cooking time needed for the bacon and garlic to caramelize and perfume the interiors. Fresh herbs, as always, will make this dish pop, as will a nice deglaze of the pan at the end to get all of the good bits up to form a sauce. This dish makes a wonderful main on its own with a little aioli, or it's a great accompaniment to roast lamb. Either way, serve a baguette and a bold white wine too.

6–8 long, slender eggplants

⅓ cup chopped fresh marjoram

Grated zest of 1–2 oranges

Kosher salt and freshly ground black pepper

12 or so cloves garlic, cut into ½-inch pieces

½ lb bacon, cut into ½-inch pieces

Extra-virgin olive oil, for drizzling

⅔ cup dry white wine

3 tablespoons butter

1 cup chopped fresh basil, plus whole leaves for garnish

1 fresh red or green chile, chopped (optional)

¼ cup chopped peeled and toasted hazelnuts, for garnish

Vincotto (see page 180) or saba, for finishing

Peppery greens, such as arugula, watercress, or mizuna, for finishing

Aioli (page 81) and toasted bread, for serving

Preheat the oven to 350°F.

Keep the eggplants whole and unpeeled, but trim off any prickles from their stems. Using a paring knife, make a pattern of small incisions all over each eggplant, making each cut about ¼ inch deep.

In a small, shallow bowl, mix together the marjoram, orange zest, and a few pinches of salt and pepper. Roll the garlic and bacon pieces in the marjoram mixture to coat them. Then, using the incisions, stud the eggplants with the bacon and garlic, alternating them in a neat pattern.

Place the eggplants in a single layer in a roasting or baking pan large enough to accommodate them without crowding. Drizzle a little oil evenly over the top and then sprinkle with salt.

Roast the eggplants until tender when pierced with a knife, 30–40 minutes.

Remove the pan from the oven, transfer the eggplants to a large serving platter, and keep warm. Place the pan on the stove top over medium heat, pour in the wine, and deglaze the pan, stirring to scrape up any bits from the pan bottom. Bring to a simmer, add the butter, basil, and chile (if using), and stir to make a sauce.

Taste the sauce, and if all is well, pour it over the eggplants. Garnish with the hazelnuts and basil, scattering them over the eggplants, and then finish with a drizzle of vincotto. Finally, dress up the platter up with a peppery green, surrounding the eggplants with the leaves.

Serve the eggplants warm, with the aioli and bread alongside.

FALL SQUASH AGRODOLCE
WITH PICKLED RAISINS, TOASTED NUTS & LABNE

■ SERVES 4–6

Have you ever asked yourself how "winter" squash got their name? We certainly have. In this book, they shall be known as "fall" squash, as only a few make it through for winter keeping. In the Northeast, we start our autumnal squash in spring, toward the end of May. They grow all summer long and are ready for harvest at the end of summer. Now what's wintry about that?

The smaller, individual-size varieties, like Delicata and Red Kuri, are the first to arrive. They do not store well, so we try to use them right away. The larger types, such as Kabocha, Long Island Cheese, and the butternut varieties, increase in flavor with a solid cure time. They are best enjoyed from late fall into early winter. One of our most prized squash varieties is the Candy Roaster. It is among the larger types we grow and definitely the most phallic in appearance. It is also one of the few Old World squash seeds that has yet to be manipulated by man. The Candy Roaster has got everything going for it: purity, flavor, a high sugar content, and zero ribs or bumps, which makes it especially easy to break down. It is a dream to cook with in the kitchen.

FOR THE PICKLED RAISINS

1 cup sultana or other raisins

1 cup aged sherry vinegar

⅓ cup water

1 teaspoon pure chile powder, such as cayenne

1 teaspoon red chile flakes

Pinch of kosher salt

—

1–2 fall squash, such as Kabocha or Red Kuri (about 6 lb total)

1 cup extra-virgin olive oil, plus more for dressing

Kosher salt and freshly ground black pepper

1–2 cups labne or crème fraîche

1 cup nuts, such as peeled hazelnuts, almonds, pecans, or pistachios, toasted until golden and chopped

Torn fresh herb leaves, such as marjoram, oregano, or flat-leaf parsley, for garnish

To make the pickled raisins, put the raisins into a small heatproof bowl. In a small saucepan, combine the vinegar, water, chile powder, chile flakes, and salt over medium heat and bring to a simmer. Remove from the heat, pour over the raisins, let sit until cool, and then set aside until using. The raisins can be prepared up to 1 week in advance, covered, and refrigerated.

Preheat the oven to 425°F. Line a large sheet pan with parchment paper.

Peel the squash, cut in half lengthwise, and scoop out and discard the seeds. Cut into wedges or other shapes that are both attractive and similar in size. Arrange in a single layer on the prepared pan and drizzle lavishly with the oil. You need a good amount of oil to ensure a glassy, crispy exterior. Season with plenty of salt and pepper.

Roast the squash pieces, giving them a flip every few minutes to ensure they cook evenly, until fork-tender, 25–30 minutes. The pieces should be nicely caramelized on the exterior and creamy on the interior.

Transfer the squash to a baking dish or wide bowl. Drain the raisins, reserving the pickling liquid, then pour a bit of the liquid over the squash along with a little olive oil to make a dressing. Season with more salt and pepper, toss to coat evenly, and let sit at room temperature for at least a couple of hours or cover and refrigerate overnight. If you choose to make this a day ahead, bring to room temperature before serving.

To serve, make a swoosh of labne on a serving platter and arrange the squash on top. Sprinkle with the raisins, nuts, and a smattering of herbs.

GRILLED CABBAGE
WITH BLACK GARLIC CAESAR

■ SERVES 4–6

Black garlic is garlic that has been put into a fermenting machine that circulates air at a specific temperature for multiple weeks. This process allows the sugars to react with the amino acids in the garlic, turning them a deep coffee brown. It is the same reaction that takes place when searing a piece of meat, known as the Maillard reaction. The flavor is distinctive and alluring, making you always want to go back for more. Black garlic can be found at farmers' markets and stores but is also easy to make at home. The tabletop fermenters can be found online and take up about the same amount of space as a rice cooker. We love to use the dark paste in aioli to accompany savory fried vegetables like Martha's Carrots (page 58) and crispy artichokes, and it will be your new best friend swiped onto toast.

FOR THE DRESSING

10–12 cloves black garlic

2–3 anchovy fillets in olive oil

About 1 cup extra-virgin olive oil

1/3 cup wine-based vinegar, such as red wine or sherry

2 tablespoons Dijon mustard

Splash of Worcestershire sauce

Kosher salt and freshly ground black pepper

—

2 petite pointed cabbages, such as Caraflex or Sweetheart, quartered or halved, depending on size, with cores trimmed but left intact

Extra-virgin olive oil, for coating

Kosher salt

FOR GARNISH

Anchovy fillets in olive oil

Toasted bread crumbs

Chopped fresh flat-leaf parsley

Toasted pine nuts

Thin shallot slices

Pinch of red chile flakes

Wedge of Parmesan cheese, for grating

To make the dressing, in the bottom of a bowl, using a fork, mash together the garlic and anchovies to a paste. Whisk in the oil, vinegar, mustard, and Worcestershire sauce until smooth, then season with salt and pepper. Taste and adjust with more oil, vinegar, or a bit of water if needed. Set aside.

Prepare a grill for direct cooking over medium-high heat. While the grill heats, coat the cabbage with olive oil and season liberally with salt.

Arrange the cabbage halves or quarters on the grill grate. Char undisturbed on each side for several minutes until nicely caramelized. Once the pieces have softened and smell sweet, transfer them to a serving platter.

Pour a liberal amount of the dressing over the cabbage (you may not need all of it). Garnish with the anchovies, bread crumbs, parsley, pine nuts, shallots, and chile flakes in amounts that suit your taste, making sure all the goodies will be included in each bite. Finish with plenty of grated Parmesan and serve right away.

TOMATO, TO-MAH-TO

Upstate New York is an area of extreme seasons, so every summer we look forward to the arrival of our first ripe tomatoes. It's hard to tell if the harsh climate of the Northeast makes them taste better or if it's just the deprivation. With the first bite of these fruits, we are reminded that the tomato, as its best, is a pure luxury and should be treated as such—in line with caviar, truffles, and fine wines. Has there ever been a type of produce as profound as the tomato? Tomato soup, tomato sauce, tomato paste, ketchup—think about it! A world without the tomato would be unrecognizable. Few, if any, ingredients can impart the same acidic and sweet flavor, let alone be the star of one of the most well-loved condiments. We as a society ought to review how we think about the tomato. These days the authenticity of a product, not its market value, is what true luxury is really about.

A Tomato a Day

At the farm, we like to enjoy tomatoes in simple preparations to a point of near exhaustion by the end of their season. We freeze cherry tomatoes whole, right off the vine, to use all winter long in sauces, soups, and breads, while we steam and process our paste tomatoes into purée.

In peak season, after a few harvests, tomatoes take on their best, most-balanced versions of themselves. They should be handled with care and with minimal adjustments. Set them on their shoulders, keeping their butts in the air, to allow them to ripen evenly. Their green hats should be kept on, too, as these help to keep them from splitting as they sit. Store them in a well-ventilated area, to keep off the flies, and at a temperature of no less than 55°F.

A Great Tomato Sandwich

- 2 slices of soft, fluffy bread, such as shokupan (Japanese milk bread) or brioche
- A few thick slabs of the best slicing tomatoes, 1/3 –1/2 inch thick
- Shower of Maldon salt and cracks of fresh black pepper
- Thick spread of Hellmann's or Best Foods mayonnaise

Press everything together into a sandwich. Eat it while standing at the cutting board and allow the juices to run down your chin.

———

A Basic, Not Basic Tomato Salad

Core a few of the most magnificent tomatoes you can find and cut them into sections. Toss the pieces into a shallow bowl and gently mix with sweet, mild raw onions. Season with a drizzle of wine vinegar and extra-virgin olive oil and a sprinkle of salt. Serve immediately. Acceptable additions include a few slices of peak-season cucumbers, bits of torn buttery olives, or sturdy, petite lettuce leaves like Little Gem.

TOMATOES WITH BROWN BUTTER

■ SERVES 4–6

When asked my favorite way to serve slicer tomatoes, I always reply, "with brown butter, black pepper, and salt." There is something about the nuttiness of brown butter that takes peak-season tomatoes to a whole new level. Our favorite tomatoes to serve this way are classified as brown tomatoes, which tend to have a meatier, more robust, umami-forward taste than green, red, or orange types. A seed called Paul Robeson has been a favorite to plant since our first year, and when combined with a decadent drizzle of brown butter, it takes on a mystical, toasty flavor. To dress this dish up, apply nothing more than a few briny capers, delicate slivers of shaved sweet onion, a scattering of earthy chanterelle mushrooms, or petite leaves of fresh basil.

8–10 tablespoons
(4–5 oz) butter

1–2 dashes sherry vinegar

Kosher salt and freshly ground
black pepper

4–6 slicer tomatoes

Maldon salt

Baguette or toast, for serving

In a sauté pan, melt the butter over medium heat. At first the butter will begin to rise and foam and then water will begin to evaporate, allowing the milk solids to darken. Watching closely, continue to cook the butter until it becomes dark brown and smells nutty. Then add the vinegar, a pinch of kosher salt, and a few cracks of pepper, stir, and remove from the heat. Set the pan aside in a warm place so the butter remains a warm liquid.

Moments before serving, slice the tomatoes about ⅓ inch thick and arrange them on a platter or individual plates. Bring the platter or plates to the table, drizzle the warm brown butter over the top, and finish with a sprinkle of Maldon salt. Apply any additional finishing touches (see headnote) and cracks of pepper. Eat the tomatoes right away while the butter is still hot. Mop up the remaining fatty juice with great bread.

PEELED TOMATOES WITH BURNT TOAST & TORN HERBS IN COLD CREAM

■ SERVES 4–6

This recipe is so stark and simple that the quality of the ingredients is of the utmost importance. Sourcing peak-season plum or other paste tomatoes and a thick, very fresh heavy cream will make all the difference. Allow your senses to take over when slipping the skins off the tomatoes as you would a silk slip. It happens to be one of my favorite things to whittle away at and becomes both addictive and sensual. This dish is a stunner on its own but also sits pretty alongside a hot (or cold) roast chicken. It is best enjoyed in early fall before summer departs, with a glass of brut Champagne or of a medium-bodied white.

About 2 cups heavy cream

Kosher salt and freshly ground black pepper

6–10 plum tomatoes (though cherry or slicing tomatoes will work too)

Extremely thin slices or shavings of nice sourdough, pumpernickel, or rye

Extra-virgin olive oil, for drizzling

1 small clove garlic

Torn or roughly chopped fresh soft herbs, such as tarragon, basil, or parsley

Maldon salt, for finishing

Season the cream well with kosher salt, cover, and refrigerate to keep very cold.

Bring a saucepan filled with water to a boil. Have ready a large bowl of ice water. Cut a small, shallow X on the bottom (blossom end) of each tomato and remove any stems. Working in batches, immerse the tomatoes in the boiling water for about 1 minute, then scoop them out and immerse them in the ice bath until cool enough to handle. Peel the tomatoes and cut away the core. Put them into a bowl and set near the stove to keep warm.

Preheat the broiler. Spread the bread pieces in a single layer on a sheet pan and drizzle with a little oil. Broil them until they have dried out and have a substantial dark char, much like burnt toast. While the pieces are still hot, gently rub the garlic clove across the top of each one in a light grating motion.

In a baking dish or deep platter that will hold the cream, arrange alternate layers of the warm tomatoes and burnt toast pieces. Pour the cream over the layers and then top with many serious cracks of black pepper and a nice scattering of herbs. Finish with Maldon salt and a drizzle of oil and serve.

DRIPPY TOMATOES
WITH MUSTARD VINAIGRETTE & AGED CHEDDAR

■ SERVES 3–4

This application should be reserved for the plumpest, most prime-season slicing tomatoes—the ones that are about to burst at the seams. The Cheddar should contain more butter than bite and carry a subtle tang to complement the sweet onion. Last but not least, whole-grain mustard—the kind that looks like seeds engulfed in gel—is a must. Garnish this wonderful dish with rosettes of mâche and a smattering of fresh basil.

FOR THE VINAIGRETTE

About ¼ cup red wine vinegar

1–2 teaspoons whole-grain mustard, such as Maille Old Style

Pinch of sugar or drizzle of runny honey

About ½ cup fruity extra-virgin olive oil

Kosher salt

—

2–4 perfectly ripe slicer tomatoes, depending on size

½ cup shaved sweet onion or poached white part of leek, in 1-inch pieces

Maldon salt and freshly ground black pepper

4–6 oz aged Cheddar cheese (Vermont's Shelburne Farms Cheddars are favorites)

Greens with some tooth, such as mâche or petite Little Gem leaves, for garnish

Handful of torn fresh basil leaves

To make the vinaigrette, in a small bowl, whisk together the vinegar, mustard, and sugar with a fork. Then slowly add the oil while whisking constantly until emulsified. Season with kosher salt and set aside.

Core the tomatoes and cut them into giant, juicy pieces of about 1½ inches thick. Arrange them in a shallow serving dish and scatter the onion over the top. Season with Maldon salt and then drizzle with the vinaigrette. Using a Microplane ribbon grater or other coarse grater, grate the Cheddar over the tomatoes, covering them from edge to edge. Top with a few cracks of pepper, garnish with greens and basil, and serve.

ROASTED CHERRY TOMATOES

- SERVES 4–6

This recipe comes in handy when you can't contain yourself from purchasing every pint of cherry tomatoes that comes into sight at the farmers' market. It is a beautiful way to preserve peak-season candy-like cherry tomatoes to enjoy later on, once their season has passed. This is also a good way to concentrate the flavors of mediocre cherry tomatoes that either aren't that sweet or are on their way out for the year. It's a win-win recipe. They are an elegant accompaniment to fried eggs and polenta, are wonderful tossed with grilled vegetables and a knob of butter for a sauce, and are delicious spooned over ricotta for scooping up with bread.

Collect the finest, sweetest cherry tomatoes from your garden, a local farm stand, or a farmers' market. The sweeter the better! Sungolds are some of our favorites, as are Rosellas. If the tomatoes you have turn out not to be the sweetest when tasted raw, you can cheat a little bit by adding a drizzle of honey or sprinkle of sugar to pump up their candy-like taste.

Word to the wise: do not discard the cooking oil! Pack the tomatoes in it to preserve them longer, toss the garlicky oil with pasta, or blend it with the tomatoes to make a sauce to serve beneath a grilled halibut fillet or a roasted pork chop.

3–4 pints cherry tomatoes

1–2 cups, very tasty extra-virgin olive oil

1 head garlic, separated into cloves, peeled, and cloves smashed

Few shallots, quartered (optional)

Drizzle of runny honey or agave syrup, if needed

Kosher salt

Handful of fresh herb sprigs

Preheat the oven to 400°F. Place the tomatoes, free of their green hats, in a single layer in a glass or ceramic baking dish or cast-iron skillet. (Cast iron will lead to the sweetest, most caramelized result.) Pour enough olive oil into the pan to cover the little butts of the tomatoes. They are by no means going for a swim, so the oil should reach no more than about one-third of the way up the sides of the tomatoes.

Slip several smashed garlic cloves in among the tomatoes. You can throw in a few quartered shallots too, and drizzle in some honey. Season the tomatoes well with salt and then tuck in some fresh herb sprigs (basil, flat-leaf parsley, thyme, and dill are good choices).

Roast the tomatoes until they begin to swell up like little balloons and crack, about 20 minutes.

Remove from the oven, let cool a bit, and then transfer the tomatoes and the oil they were cooked in to glass jars. If they are not fully submerged in oil, add more as needed to cover. Cover tightly and refrigerate. They will keep in the fridge for a few weeks, but I can almost guarantee you'll eat them up before then.

MY MOM'S TOMATO-MOZZARELLA PASTA

- **SERVES 4–6**

You cannot beat the combination of flavors in this dish. The aroma of it transports me back to dewy summer evenings spent by the pool as a child. It is a favorite meal of my mother's to prepare and also for anyone else who encounters it. The marinated mixture of marshmallow-like mozzarella and candy-sweet tomatoes is hard not to devour while you wait for the pasta to cook. My mother will probably read this and tell me that I've overcomplicated her recipe, proclaiming that she would never use a grater for the garlic, only a garlic press. I will agree to disagree.

---

2 lb of the best, sweetest tomatoes you can find

1 cup fresh basil leaves, torn or roughly chopped, plus more for garnish

2–4 cups cut-up fresh whole-milk mozzarella cheese, in 1-inch nuggets (or ciliegine size)

2–4 cloves garlic, grated

¾ cup extra-virgin olive oil, plus more if needed

¼ cup white wine vinegar, or more or less to taste

Runny honey for drizzling or a pinch of sugar, if needed

Kosher salt and freshly ground black pepper

1–1½ lb dried pasta, such as pappardelle, fettuccine, or tagliatelle

Red chile flakes, for serving

Wedge of Parmesan cheese, for serving

Cut the tomatoes into bite-size pieces. If using cherry tomatoes, simply cut them in half. If using large tomatoes, squeeze out and discard the seeds to reduce the water content, but don't be too obsessive about it.

In a large bowl, combine the tomatoes, basil, and as much mozzarella and garlic as you like. Pour in the oil and vinegar. If your tomatoes are not very sweet, drizzle in a little honey or a sprinkle of sugar. Season with salt and pepper. Give everything a good stir and then leave at room temperature for about 30 minutes.

Bring a large pot of water to a boil and add a fistful of salt. Pasta water should be salty like the sea to season the pasta properly. Add the pasta and cook, stirring occasionally, until al dente, according to the package directions. Drain into a colander, then return the pasta to the warm pot off the heat.

Add the tomato-mozzarella mixture to the hot pasta and fold in gently, coating the pasta evenly and adjusting with a bit more oil if needed for a good ratio of pasta to sauce. Taste and adjust the seasoning with salt and pepper if needed, then plate up in shallow bowls, giving each guest some extra-gooey, barely melted mozzarella chunks and juicy tomatoes on top.

Top each serving with a few more basil leaves and serve right away. Offer chile flakes and a giant hunk of Parmesan cheese for grating at the table.

40 CLOVES OF GARLIC CHICKEN
WITH CARROTS, ONIONS & POTATOES

■ SERVES 4–6

Although chicken might seem like it wants to be the star of this dish, I can promise you it doesn't stand a chance. Garlic has been a star crop in recent years—a rebel without a seed packet because its seeds are the cloves! It obeys a growing schedule opposite of most everything else due to its need for a deep cold rest. Planting thousands of cloves in early October produces beautiful garlic heads for us by the following July. We grow a hardneck variety named German White, which we originally sourced from the Maine Potato Lady, a wonderful garlic and potato purveyor in the far Northeast. Garlic grows as a clone, so over the years, we have saved the most prime cloves from some of the heads to create our own seed stock to ensure premium results. Our harvest has a clean, bright flavor and four to six meaty cloves per head, which makes for easy peeling. Quality garlic is key to this recipe, so source some from your local farmers' market rather than the supermarket.

We find many uses at home for the cloves from heads that don't make it into our seed stock. Using forty cloves for one chicken may seem excessive, but when garlic is exposed to prolonged cooking, it mellows, leaving the most comforting and intoxicating scent and flavor. This dish is perfectly suited to a house warmed by a roaring fire on a cold winter night. Serve with ample amounts of cold salty butter and baguette. For a nice pairing, pour a red wine with a light-medium body or a dry, big white.

---

12 bone-in, skin-on chicken thighs and drumsticks, or 1 whole chicken, about 4 lb, cut into serving pieces

Kosher salt

1 lb waxy potatoes, cut into 2-inch pieces if large

3–4 carrots, cut into 1- to 2-inch pieces

1 large yellow onion, chopped

Extra-virgin olive oil, for drizzling

1 cup dry vermouth or white wine, plus more if needed

40 cloves garlic, unpeeled but cleaned of excess papery skin

½ cup (4 oz) butter, cut into pieces

Few fresh thyme sprigs

Freshly grated nutmeg, for sprinkling

Sweet paprika, for sprinkling

Baguette, for serving

Coat the chicken pieces with about 2 teaspoons salt, put them into a large bowl, cover the bowl, and let sit in the refrigerator for about 1 hour. Then drain off the liquid that has collected at the bottom and set the chicken aside.

Preheat the oven to 400°F. Put the potatoes, carrots, and onion into a large roasting pan. Drizzle them with a bit of oil, sprinkle with salt, and toss until they have a very light sheen. Place the chicken pieces, skin side up, in the pan, arranging them in among the vegetables, and drizzle them with a little oil. Pour the vermouth into the pan, then tuck in the garlic cloves, butter pieces, and thyme. Sprinkle the nutmeg and paprika over the chicken and vegetables.

Cover the pan with aluminum foil, place in the oven, and bake for about 1 hour. Remove the foil and continue to bake until the chicken is cooked through and the skin begins to brown, about 30 minutes longer, adding a little more vermouth if needed to prevent sticking.

Remove from the oven and let cool slightly before serving. Serve this radiant dish with sliced baguette alongside, encouraging diners to slip the garlic cloves from their skins, and smear them on top of the bread along with the sweet, buttery carrots.

GARLICKY BROCCOLI RABE
WITH HABANADA PESTO & BREAD CRUMBS

- **SERVES 4–8**

We grew broccoli rabe during our first spring at the start of the pandemic in 2020. The seed name, Quarentina, proved to be an ironic and comical addition to our field plot. We were excited about the prospect of growing broccoli rabe that was less bitter than the commonly found bunches in the grocery store. They are typically extra bitter and have a superfluous number of leaves that are unpalatable. When our first harvest was ready, we were blown away by the difference—the subtlest amount of bitter, the most sweet and juicy crunch. When blanched, the green tones could blind the eye with their vibrancy. Much like other vegetables that contain bitter notes, broccoli rabe is best when grown in cooler seasons, as the chill brings its sugars forward and mellows the bite. If you can find only the extra-bitter stuff, substitute baby broccoli, broccolini, or flowering cauliflower. The pesto calls for tangerine-hued Habanada peppers, which are basically habaneros but without the fire, and buttery Marcona almonds. Use a really nice olive oil for best results.

FOR THE BROCCOLI RABE

4 bunches tender, sweet broccoli rabe (about 2 lb total)

Extra-virgin olive oil, for cooking

2 cloves garlic, finely chopped

Knob of butter

Kosher salt

Habanada Pesto (page 222)

FOR THE GARNISH

Extra-Crunchy Garlicky Bread Crumbs (page 115) or toasted bread crumbs

Torn fresh flat-leaf parsley leaves

Few lemon cheeks

To prepare the broccoli rabe, trim and blanch the broccoli rabe as directed on page 18, pulling it out of the hot water and rapidly plunging it into the ice bath to keep a nice crunch. Drain well and pat dry.

Cover the bottom of a large sauté pan with oil and place over medium heat. Add the garlic and cook, stirring often, until light golden, about 5 minutes. Add the broccoli rabe and butter and sauté until tender, about 5 minutes. Season with salt and remove from the heat.

To serve, line up the broccoli rabe like soldiers on a platter. Dollop the pesto in a line across the middle of the stalks. Garnish with a dusting of bread crumbs, a scattering of parsley, and the lemon cheeks and serve.

BUTTER-GLAZED AVOCADO SQUASH
WITH CHILES, CACIOCAVALLO, CRUNCHIES & GARLIC CHIVES

- SERVES 4–6

Many years ago, while running my restaurants in NYC, I would go on the hunt for spectacular produce at the Union Square Greenmarket. One day, I came across a variety of summer squash from Bodhi Tree Farm labeled avocado squash. Its true name is Early Bulam, and it is a hybridized squash seed of Korean descent. It has an uncanny resemblance to a bright green avocado with a gradient green flesh, thus its nickname. Even its nutty flavors whisper a likeness to the creamy fruit. A prolific squash seed to be discovered and enjoyed!

Do not fret should you not be able to find this variety, as a mix of summer squashes can be substituted. In fact, using a variety of summer squashes can be a good thing because their flavors and textures are often very different, making this dish interesting and fun. Serve it alongside grilled chicken or sweet Italian sausage and a refreshingly tart salad. Chardonnay is a nice pairing to contrast with the richness of the butter and cheese.

5–7 small-to-medium avocado squashes, about 3 lb total

¾ cup (6 oz) butter

½ cup water

Kosher salt and freshly ground black pepper

Drizzle of runny honey or pinch of sugar

1–2 fresh red chiles with moderate heat, such as Fresno, seeded if too hot and thinly sliced

½ cup chopped fresh garlic chives

¼ lb caciocavallo, toma, or other mild, melty cheese

½ cup Extra-Crunchy Garlicky Bread Crumbs (page 115) or toasted panko bread crumbs

Torn fresh basil leaves, for garnish

HOT TIP The butter-glazed squash makes for a great pasta dish. Chop the squash into slightly smaller pieces and toss with al dente noodles, cooked Italian sausage, and loads of torn fresh basil.

Trim off the ends from each squash and slice the squash into orange-section-like segments.

In a large sauté pan over low heat, melt the butter. Add the squash and water and raise the heat to a simmer. Add a pinch of salt, a crack of pepper, and the honey, stir once, cover the pan, and let the liquid simmer for a minute or so. Uncover the pan and continue to simmer until the squash pieces are tender and the liquid is reduced to a shiny glaze around the pieces, about 10 minutes.

Add the chiles and then most of the chives, reserving a little for garnish, and toss to combine. Transfer the contents of the pan to a platter. Using a Microplane ribbon grater or the large holes of a box grater, shred the cheese over the top in thick strands that will melt slightly from the heat of the squash. Follow with the bread crumbs, the remaining chives, lots of basil, and a few grinds of pepper and serve.

BUTTERED GREEN BEANS
WITH MORTADELLA, PICKLED CARROTS & CRISPY SHALLOTS

■ SERVES 4–6

Let's take a moment and pay some respect to beans and the people who grow them. In our experience, beans are one of the most time-consuming vegetables to grow. They need more attention from the get-go because they are directly seeded into the ground during spring and the weeds *love* them. There are bush varieties that grow low and compact, making for a backbreaking harvest, and there are pole varieties that grow upward in a more singular fashion. They all need a tremendous amount of care and time. For whatever reason, society has become accustomed to the idea that beans should be low in price and casually treated. Well, I am here to tell you that they ought to be top dollar for the amount of work they require! We do not attempt them every year, but when we do, they are an exhausting and delicious delight. #respectthebean

---

2–3 carrots (see Hot Tip)

½ cup sherry or champagne vinegar

Large pinch each of kosher salt and sugar

1½–2 lb petite green beans

Butter, for cooking

6–8 oz mortadella, diced

1 shallot, diced or sliced

Dry white wine, vermouth, or fresh lemon juice, for deglazing

Freshly grated nutmeg, for seasoning and garnish

Crispy Shallots, for garnish (page 179)

Chopped fresh flat-leaf parsley, for garnish

Freshly ground black pepper and/or grated Parmesan cheese, for garnish

HOT TIP You can skip pickling the carrots and instead buy a jar of lacto-fermented pickled carrot sticks, chop them into nice pieces, and scatter them on top of the beans.

Using a vegetable peeler or mandoline, shave the carrots lengthwise into ribbons and put into a bowl. In a small saucepan, heat the vinegar, salt, and sugar over medium heat then pour the warm liquid over the carrots to give them a quick pickle. Set aside while you cook the beans, then drain just before using.

Trim the green beans, then blanch as directed on page 18. They will undergo more cooking later on, so dunk them into the boiling water only briefly, then plunge them into the ice bath to cool. Drain well and pat dry.

In a sauté pan large enough to accommodate the green beans, melt a few tablespoons of butter—be generous—over medium heat. Add the mortadella and shallot and give them just a light sauté, 1–2 minutes. Add a little wine and deglaze the pan, scraping up any bits from the pan bottom. Throw in a pinch of salt and a few grates of nutmeg and then add the green beans, a little more butter, and a touch of water. Reduce until the water and butter become emulsified, forming a creamy sheen, and the green beans are tender but still have a bit of tooth. Taste for salt and correct if needed, then immediately remove from the heat.

Arrange the green beans on a platter, topping them with the beautiful frilly pickled carrot ribbons, copious amounts of crispy shallots, and some chopped parsley. A little more nutmeg and some pepper and/or Parmesan are also nice. Serve right away.

CABBAGE AU POIVRE

■ SERVES 4–6

A classic French treatment for a steak that can be lovely or deadly. Many times au poivre is executed with no finesse: overt hunks of black peppercorns are pressed into the sides of a steak only to burn during the sear, leaving the eater choking later on. I've been there, and it's awkward. In this graceful approach, the tangy cream sauce kisses briny and floral green peppercorns in the pan. Then the sauce is finished with a robust, fine grind of black pepper.

The commonly served beef is swapped out for petite wedges of cabbage that have been brined overnight to become meaty and juicy in texture. Serve with a side of thinly cut French fries or Crispy Fried Larattes (page 170). Choose a jammy, fruit-forward red wine to complement the peppery sauce.

FOR THE CABBAGE

6–8 cups water

Kosher salt and freshly fine-ground black pepper

¼ cup honey

2 tablespoons black peppercorns

2 petite pointed cabbages, such as Caraflex or Sweetheart, quartered or halved, with cores trimmed but left intact

⅓ cup grapeseed or canola oil

FOR THE SAUCE

½ cup (4 oz) butter

2 plump shallots, sliced

2–3 tablespoons green peppercorns in brine, drained

½ cup Cognac, plus more for finishing

1 cup crème fraîche

1 tablespoon Dijon mustard

Splash of heavy cream or vegetable stock, for thinning

Kosher salt and freshly ground black pepper

½ cup fresh flat-leaf parsley leaves, roughly chopped, plus more for garnish

To brine the cabbage, in a large saucepan over high heat, combine the water, ⅓ cup salt, honey, and black peppercorns and bring to a boil, stirring occasionally. Add the cabbage pieces, turn off the heat, let cool, and then transfer the brine and cabbages to a covered container and refrigerate overnight.

The next day, remove the cabbages from the brine and discard the brine. Give the cabbages a gentle squeeze with a kitchen towel to release excess moisture, then arrange them in a single layer on a platter or tray and let air-dry at room temperature for a couple of hours. This ensures they will take on an epic sear when they hit the hot pan.

Once the cabbages are dry on the outside, season them lightly with salt and a few grinds of pepper. In a large sauté pan, heat the oil over high heat until shimmering. Add the cabbage pieces, cut side down, and cook undisturbed for a few minutes to ensure a deep caramelization before turning them. Continue to cook until they become soft and meaty yet still retain their shape and are caramelized on all sides, 20–30 minutes. Transfer the cabbage pieces to a platter and keep warm.

To make the sauce, dump out any oil remaining in the sauté pan and return the pan to the stove top over medium heat. Add the butter and shallots (and perhaps some minced garlic too if you fancy) and sweat, stirring now and again, until soft, about 2 minutes. Add the green peppercorns and stir well. Carefully pour in the Cognac and deglaze the pan, scraping up any bits from the bottom. Add the crème fraîche and mustard, swirl the pan until the mixture emulsifies, and then thin it out with a bit of cream. Crack in an abundance of black pepper while swirling the pan and finish with a little salt. The final touches are a fistful of parsley and a drop more Cognac for an added kick, swirling to mix.

Spoon the sauce over the cabbages, finishing with more pepper cracks and parsley. Serve right away.

BLANCHED SAVOY CABBAGE WITH WALNUTS

■ SERVES 4–6

Cabbage has earned a somewhat bad reputation for getting served overcooked, underseasoned, and brimming with unpleasant sewage-like notes. This dish proves all of that wrong. Blanched crinkly Savoy leaves take on a freshness and richness when combined with toasted walnuts and bright lemon, making for an addictive side or beginning to a meal.

   The Parmesan and bread crumbs added at the end ensure all the textures pop and should not be skipped. Nor should you skimp on the olive oil, which creeps into the cabbage pores and makes it really juicy.

1–2 heads Savoy cabbage

1–2 cups extra-virgin olive oil, plus more for drizzling

Juice of 1–3 lemons

Kosher salt and freshly ground black pepper

½ cup walnuts, toasted and chopped

½ cup torn fresh flat-leaf parsley leaves

1 small shallot, thinly sliced

½ cup grated Parmesan cheese

½ cup toasted bread crumbs

Cut each cabbage in half through the stem end to expose the core. Remove and discard the core from each half with a paring knife and then separate the leaves.

Have ready a large bowl of ice water. Bring a large, wide pot filled with water to a boil over high heat. Season it liberally with salt until it tastes like the sea. Add the cabbage leaves and blanch for about 1 minute, then immediately transfer the leaves to the ice bath to cool. Drain and pat completely dry. Place in a large bowl.

Add the oil and lemon juice to the leaves, using just enough to coat and flavor the leaves lightly, and season with salt and pepper. Toss to mix evenly, then gently massage the marinade into the leaves with care. The leaves can be used right away or left to hang close by in the refrigerator for up to 1 hour.

When ready to serve, add the walnuts, parsley, and shallot and mix to combine. Check for seasoning and adjust if needed.

Layer some of the cabbage leaves and their goodies on a platter and strew some of the Parmesan and bread crumbs evenly on top for depth and crunch. Top with another layer of leaves and more Parmesan and bread crumbs. Repeat until you have used all the ingredients. Finish with a drizzle of oil and serve.

CUCUMBERS WITH ONIONS & HERBS

- **SERVES 4–6**

If you don't grow your own cucumbers, we highly recommend a visit to your farmers' market to gather a mix of varieties, such as Dragon's Egg, Katrina, and Lemon, for this dish. They all have their own unique flavor profile and texture, and when brought together, they can make a mundane salad sing. Because of the simplicity of this dish, the quality of the cucumbers will either make it or break it. We love the sweetness and floral qualities of a moscatel vinegar, but rice vinegar with a dash of red wine vinegar is a fine substitute. Just make sure whatever vinegar you use isn't too harsh on the throat because it will mask the beautiful cucumber flavor. If you cannot find spring (fresh) onions, use shallots in their place.

---

2 lb assorted cucumbers
(see headnote)

Few pinches of kosher salt
(about 1 tablespoon)

Few pinches of sugar
(about 1 tablespoon)

⅓ cup or so moscatel vinegar

Couple of glugs of extra-virgin
olive oil

1–2 mild spring (fresh) onions,
such as Tropeana Lunga,
thinly sliced

Assorted fresh soft herbs, such
as basil, dill, and mint, chopped,
for garnish

Peel any cucumbers that have tough unappetizing skin, then cut up the cucumbers in a variety of fun bite-size shapes. Transfer them to a bowl and toss with the salt and sugar, which will help them release their water. Let the cucumbers sit for about 20 minutes and then drain off the water that has collected at the bottom of the bowl.

Add the vinegar, oil, and onions and toss to mix evenly. Let sit for 10–20 minutes more. Just before serving, check the seasoning and adjust if needed. Garnish with loads of herbs and serve.

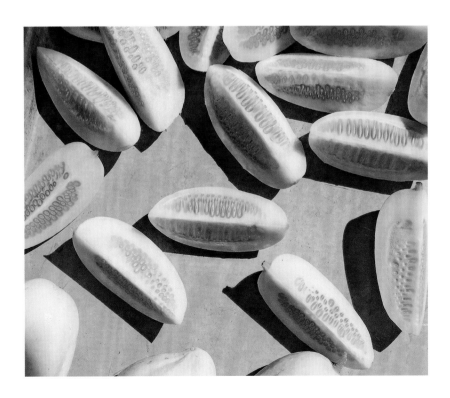

UNCLE FREDO'S ASPARAGUS

■ SERVES 4–6

Any vegetable is bound to be great coated with Parmesan cheese and brown butter. Here, in true Fredo style, juicy asparagus stalks are prepared as shown to us by our Uncle Fredo, a dish passed down to him by his mom. Simply said, it's *fabulous*!

---

2 bunches asparagus, trimmed of woody ends

Wedge of Parmesan cheese (3–4 oz)

8–10 tablespoons butter

Maldon salt and freshly ground black pepper

HOT TIP An update to this dish finds Manchego to be an excellent alternative (if not a better option) to the Parmesan.

Blanch the asparagus stalks as directed on page 18 until they are tender but still have crunch, then shock in the ice bath until cool. Drain well.

Lay the asparagus on an impressive serving platter. Grate an abundant amount of Parmesan cheese—about 1 cup—over them and let sit at room temperature while you prepare the butter.

In a sauté pan, melt the butter over medium heat. At first the butter will foam and then the milk solids will begin to brown at the bottom of the pan. Watching closely, continue to heat, stirring occasionally, until the milk solids turn a deep chocolate brown and the butter smells nutty, then remove from the heat.

Pour the hot butter over the platter that awaits, melting the snowy cheese covering the stalks. Sprinkle with salt and several twists of pepper and serve immediately with tongs.

CAST-IRON JAPANESE SWEET POTATOES

■ SERVES 6–8

Sweet potatoes are a very high-maintenance plant to grow. They are a member of the morning glory family—and no, they are not the same as a yam! The yam and the sweet potato actually belong to two entirely different botanical families. The yam, hailing from Africa, was brought to the United States during the transatlantic slave trade. It was a top crop in Africa and quite similar to cassava root. Some people think the yam looks like the sweet potato, which is native to North America, and thus have equated the two.

There are many sweet potato varieties, but our favorite is the Japanese sweet potato, which has deep pink skin and supersweet white flesh. We like to serve them hot and crispy with a swath of labne or a savory citrus zabaglione. Topping them with a generous drizzle of homemade salsa verde (pages 220–221) makes for a spectacularly punchy garnish.

4–6 Japanese sweet potatoes, not too big and preferably uniform in size, halved lengthwise

Kosher salt

¼ cup extra-virgin olive oil

2–3 tablespoons butter

Preheat the oven to 400°F.

Liberally season the sweet potatoes all over with salt. Place a cast-iron skillet large enough to hold the sweet potatoes in a single layer over medium-high heat and add the oil and butter. When the butter has melted and the butter and oil are nice and hot, place the potatoes cut side down in the pan and do not move them! Cook for a few minutes until the cut sides start to take on a nice caramel color.

Transfer the pan to the oven and bake until the sweet potatoes are fork-tender, 30–35 minutes. Serve right away.

CRISPY FRIED LARATTES
WITH AIOLI & GOODNESS

■ SERVES 4–6

Laratte is a prized French fingerling variety that we grew with great excitement in our very first year on the farm, and we still use the same Maine purveyor to source the beautiful seed potatoes. The variety is sought after by many chefs for its buttery flavor and silky texture, and though the potatoes grow into a range of sizes, their flavor and texture are always consistent, which is rare. They take a bit longer to grow in our area than other new-type potatoes and do not store well, so they must be used quite soon after harvest. Boiled and tossed with salty butter is the easiest and quickest way to enjoy their luxury. If you have a bit more patience, they are also wonderful puréed (page 128).

Frying them up after a boil in water becomes magical with a thick aioli served alongside. A few radiant goodies can be tossed in among them, but be careful not to overpower them. The simplest additions, such as torn herbs and bits of crispy ham or a few mild, buttery torn olives, are usually best. On other occasions, crème fraîche and caviar with wisps of shallot and parsley are welcome partners. However you decide to finish them, they should always have a sumptuous simplicity and glassy crunch.

2–3 lb Laratte or other fingerling potatoes

Kosher salt

1–2 cups oil or fat, such as grapeseed, canola, or olive oil or rendered chicken or duck fat

In a large pot, combine the potatoes, a fistful of salt, and water to cover. Place over medium heat, bring to a boil, and cook until the potatoes are fork-tender but not falling apart. The timing will vary depending on their size, but they are usually ready in 25–30 minutes.

Drain the potatoes and arrange them in a single layer on a large sheet pan (or two smaller sheet pans). Let cool until they can be handled with a bare hand, then, using the bottom of a cup, a small pan, or other flat-bottomed object, press on each potato to make it a squat version of itself but not nearly a pancake. It's fine if large crumbs or nuggets break off. This can be done a day in advance; cover and refrigerate until ready to continue.

Pour the oil or rendered fat into a medium cast-iron or other heavy pot and heat to 350°F. The oil or fat should be 1–3 inches deep depending on the size of your potatoes (you want them to be submerged). Line a large plate with paper towels and set it near the stove.

When the oil or fat is hot, working in batches, add the potatoes and fry, turning as needed, until crispy and golden brown, 5–7 minutes, rotating as needed so the entire exterior becomes a nice even golden brown. As each batch is done, using tongs, transfer the potatoes to the towel-lined plate to drain. Toss the potatoes with a shower of salt while they are still warm, then garnish as desired (see headnote) and serve.

GOLDEN MELTING POTATOES

■ SERVES 6–8

Known in French cuisine as pommes de terre fondantes, these potato nuggets are one of the most impressive classic French potato recipes—and one of the easiest. They can be prepared with little effort on a random Wednesday night for serving with roasted chicken or on New Year's Eve for proudly displaying around a standing rib roast.

Butter alone will always do more than just fine for this preparation, but if you want to kick it up a notch, use rendered animal fat for the searing and basting. Fats like beef tallow, bacon drippings, duck fat, or schmaltz all yield fabulous results. A gelatinous bone broth or stock is key to the potatoes achieving a creamy melted texture and to the final emulsification of the sauce.

As for the potatoes, starchy russets will work, but the waxy varieties tend to hold their shape better when prepared this way. If you only have russets, carry on! A cast-iron sauté pan is preferred, but a stainless-steel pan will work well too. Just make sure the sides are straight rather than sloping to contain the liquid and steam. Finally, please execute this recipe with equal parts confidence and caution, as the hot fat often pops and splatters. Donning kitchen goggles or glasses is recommended.

---

4 lb potatoes (see headnote)

¼ cup extra-virgin olive oil or rendered animal fat

Kosher salt

8–10 tablespoons (4–5 oz) butter

6–8 cloves garlic

Several fresh thyme, oregano, marjoram, or rosemary sprigs, plus chopped herbs for garnish

Splash of dry white wine

3–4 cups bone broth or stock (the best you can find)

Maldon salt and freshly ground black pepper

Preheat the oven to 450°F.

Peel the potatoes, then cut them into sea scallop–like pieces with flattened sides and pat them dry. Place a large, heavy sauté pan over medium heat. Add the oil and heat until very hot and slightly smoking. (If you do not have a pan that is large enough, brown the potatoes in batches.)

Season the potatoes with a liberal coating of kosher salt and then place directly in the hot oil. Do not move these nuggets for about 5 minutes to allow a deep sear to develop. Instead, gently rotate the pan to swirl the oil around the pieces. When the underside is a dark golden brown, using a spatula, flip them again and cook undisturbed until the second side is a dark golden brown.

Once both sides are nicely seared, add the butter, garlic cloves, and herb sprigs. When the butter melts and foams, cook for a minute or two longer. Add the wine and deglaze the pan, carefully stirring to dislodge any bits on the bottom. Pour in the broth and bring to a boil. Transfer the pan to the oven and cook until the potatoes offer no resistance when pierced with a knife and the liquid has thickened, 35–40 minutes.

Return the pan to the stove top, transfer the potatoes to a platter, and reduce the sauce further over medium heat until it is shiny and emulsified. If it appears to separate, add a little water or oil and bring it back together, then cook for another minute.

Spoon the sauce over the potatoes and finish with Maldon salt, pepper, and chopped herbs. Serve immediately.

POBLANOS STUFFED WITH CHEESY GREEN CHILE RICE

■ SERVES 4–6

We adore growing peppers of all types, from hot to sweet, and use the varieties we cultivate to make many value-added products, from powders to hot sauces. Our poblano plants are among our most prolific pepper plants, and we typically enjoy the peppers right off the plant, simply prepared. They are also the earliest to arrive, ready for picking in July, while we must wait until mid-September for other peppers.

Poblanos are versatile, good in salsas, soups, and chili or shaved on pizza for quick cooking in a hot oven. They have the perfect amount of mild heat, a bright vegetal flavor, and are the ideal size for stuffing. For this dish, plan on two or three poblano halves per diner, depending on the size of the chiles. Fresh Hatch chiles are great to use in the stuffing, or you can also use more poblano chiles or even good-quality canned chiles. Accompany the stuffed poblanos with a bowl of fresh salsa and well-chilled, stiff margaritas (page 32).

4–8 poblano chiles, depending on size, with stems intact

Fresh salsa and lime wedges, for serving

FOR THE FILLING

3 cups cooked short-grain brown rice, at room temperature

1 heaping cup charred chopped green chiles (see headnote)

1 cup chopped green onions, white and green parts

1 cup chopped fresh cilantro leaves and stems

1 clove garlic, grated

4 oz cream cheese, at room temperature

½ cup labne, sour cream, or crème fraîche

½ cup shredded Jack cheese, plus more for topping

½ cup shredded Cheddar cheese, plus more for topping

1–2 teaspoons cumin seeds, toasted and crushed

Kosher salt and freshly ground black pepper

Preheat the oven to 375°F. Line a sheet pan with aluminum foil.

Split each poblano in half lengthwise, leaving the stem intact on one of the halves. Remove and discard the seeds and membranes and set the chile halves aside.

To make the filling, in a medium bowl, combine the rice, chopped chiles, green onions, cilantro, garlic, cream cheese, labne, Jack and Cheddar cheeses, 1 teaspoon of the cumin, a big pinch of salt, and a few twists of pepper and mix well. Taste and adjust the seasoning with cumin, salt, and pepper if needed.

Stuff each pepper cavity with the rice mixture and top with a little Jack and Cheddar cheese. Arrange the stuffed chiles on the prepared pan.

Bake until the filling is bubbly, the tops are browned, and the peppers are tender, about 30 minutes. Serve warm with the salsa and lime wedges.

HOT TIP If you don't want to stuff poblanos, the rice mixture also makes a lovely dish on its own. Spoon it into a generously buttered baking dish, top with a little more Jack and Cheddar cheese, and bake at 375°F until bubbly and browned, about 20 minutes.

EGGPLANT STEAKS
WITH ROASTED CHERRY TOMATOES, PINE NUTS & SOUBISE

■ SERVES 4–6

Onions are front and center in soubise, one of the great French white sauces. It is silky, slightly sweet, and supremely savory. We use our Cippolini onions for a nice white, but any hue of onion will suffice. The sauce pairs terrifically with all meat and fish, but we love it most served beneath oven-roasted eggplant steaks topped with roasted cherry tomatoes. It can be used in recipes that call for béchamel, like our Tarte Flambée (page 131), but it has a lighter taste because it is finished with just a touch of cream.

FOR THE SOUBISE

About ½ cup (8 oz) butter and/or extra-virgin olive oil

1½–2 lb cippolini or other onion of choice, chopped or sliced

Kosher salt

2–3 splashes of dry white wine (optional)

About ½ cup heavy cream

Pinch of freshly ground white pepper (optional)

FOR THE EGGPLANT

4–6 globe eggplants, about 2–3 lb

Extra-virgin olive oil, for drizzling

Kosher salt

Roasted Cherry Tomatoes (page 149), for garnish

Toasted pine nuts, for garnish

Torn or chopped fresh herbs of choice, for garnish

HOT TIP To make a vegan soubise, which admittedly comes out great, too, replace the cream with a good extra-virgin olive oil to give a nice fatty mouthfeel and a drop of water to thin the sauce to a good consistency.

To make the soubise, place a large sauté pan over medium heat, add the butter and/or oil and the onions and toss in a couple of pinches of salt so the onions release their moisture. Sweat the onions, stirring occasionally, until soft, 20–30 minutes. Add the wine, if using, and cook for another minute or so to mellow.

Transfer the onions to a blender. With the blender on high speed, stream in the cream just until you have a smooth purée. The consistency should be thicker than soup but thinner than a potato purée.

Taste and adjust the salinity if needed and add the white pepper if you feel it fits. Pass the sauce through a fine-mesh sieve for an ultra-silky consistency. You should have about 2 cups. Set aside.

To make the eggplant, preheat the oven to 425°F if using the convection setting or 450°F if using a conventional oven. Line a large sheet pan with parchment paper or a nonstick baking mat.

Trim off the stem and blossom end of each eggplant, then peel the eggplants lengthwise. Cut each eggplant into rounds about 3 inches thick. Arrange the rounds in a single layer, not touching, on the prepared pan. Drizzle the tops liberally with olive oil and season with salt, then give them a flip and do the same on the opposite side.

Bake the eggplant rounds until golden on the outside and tender when pierced with a knife tip, 25–30 minutes. Remove from the oven and let cool slightly before handling.

Spoon the soubise onto a large platter or plate. Nestle the warm eggplant steaks in the sauce and then spoon the cherry tomatoes around the slices. Garnish with the pine nuts and herbs and serve.

CREAMY GREEN POLENTA
WITH FRIED EGGS & CRISPY SHALLOTS

■ SERVES 6

Corn, much like beans, is grown from seeds that have been easy to transport in a pocket over time. Many pockets on many journeys have produced many stories. However there remains an abundance of corn varieties with rich histories that have never been commodified. Every region has many historically specific varieties with their own best uses. Some are better for popping, others are better for grinding, and still others are best suited for alcohol.

We don't often grow corn on the farm, especially sweet corn, but when we do, we always choose hardy and unique varieties. We have tried tiny-kernel popping varieties, like black and strawberry popcorns, along with milling corns, such as Hopi Blue and Oaxacan Green Dent. We have also worked with local breweries to make beautiful Mexican-style lagers with our corn in the ferment. Depending on the grind of the corn you have, larger grinds might need a day of soaking before cooking, much like dried beans.

FOR THE GREEN PURÉE

Extra-virgin olive oil, for cooking and puréeing

1 lb greens of choice, such as Tuscan (lacinato) kale, komatsuna (Japanese mustard spinach), or spinach, tough stems removed

1 shallot, thinly sliced

Pinch of red chile flakes

Kosher salt and freshly ground black pepper

Pinch of grated lemon zest

FOR THE POLENTA

⅓ cup extra-virgin olive oil

1–3 cloves garlic, chopped

4 cups whole milk, heavy cream, or water and/or broth for a dairy-free version, plus more as needed

2 cups water

Splash of dry white wine

Kosher salt and freshly ground black pepper

To make the green purée, cover the bottom of a large sauté pan with olive oil, place over medium heat, and add the greens, shallot, and a spoonful or two of water. Cook, stirring often, until the greens are wilted. Timing will vary depending on the green used. Season with the chile flakes and salt and pepper and remove from the heat.

Transfer the greens to a food processor, add the lemon zest, and process to a smooth purée, adding a little oil if needed to achieve a good consistency. Check the seasoning, adjust if needed, and set aside. (You will have more than you need for the polenta. The remainder will keep in a covered container in the refrigerator for up to 1 week and can be used to top eggs and pasta.)

To make the polenta, pick a saucepan that anticipates growth, place over medium heat, and pour in the oil. Add the garlic and cook, stirring often, until golden brown, about 8 minutes; do not allow it to burn. Add the milk, water, wine, and a hefty pinch of salt and bring to a simmer, keeping a close eye so it doesn't boil over.

Once the milk mixture is simmering, add the polenta in a streaming pour while whisking constantly. Then continue to whisk and simmer the mixture for a few minutes until it thickens slightly to a porridge consistency. Add half of the butter and continue to simmer, whisking often, for another 10 minutes or so, then turn off the heat. Cover the pan with a tight-fitting lid or aluminum foil and keep on the warm stove for about 30 minutes so the grains have a chance to absorb the liquid.

1 cup polenta or grits

¾ cup (6 oz) butter

½ cup green purée

1 cup grated Manchego, Parmesan, Cheddar, or aged Gouda cheese (optional)

Grated lemon zest (optional)

—

Fried eggs (any style) cooked in butter, for serving

Crispy Shallots, for garnish

Chile oil, for garnish

Torn fresh herb leaves of choice, for garnish

Check the polenta and adjust with more milk or broth or water if it is too thick. It should be the consistency of porridge. Stir in the remaining butter and the green purée, then taste for seasoning and adjust if needed. If you like, fold in the cheese and perhaps a bit of lemon zest.

Plate the polenta in wide bowls and top with the fried eggs. Garnish with crispy shallots, a drizzle of fragrant chile oil, and a dusting of herbs and serve at once.

CRISPY SHALLOTS

Makes about 2 cups

Using a mandoline, cut 3 or 4 shallots crosswise into thin slices. Drop the slices into a bowl and toss them with your fingers, separating all the rings. Pour about ¾ cup whole milk or buttermilk over the shallot rings and let soak for 15–20 minutes.

Pour grapeseed, canola, or other neutral oil to a depth of about 2 inches into a small, deep, heavy pan and heat to 350°F. Line a plate with paper towels and set near the stove. When the oil is ready, drain the shallots, allowing the excess milk to drip off, and dredge them in about 1 cup all-purpose flour seasoned with kosher salt and freshly ground black pepper (or cayenne pepper), tapping off the excess. Add the shallots to the hot oil and fry until golden brown, 4–5 minutes. Scoop out the shallots with a spider and drain on the towel-lined plate. Season the crisp shallot rings with a nice amount of salt while they are still hot. Eat within a couple of hours or immediately after frying if it's humid outside.

HAKUREI TURNIPS
WITH SWEET ITALIAN SAUSAGE, PARMESAN & VINCOTTO

■ SERVES 4–6

Do yourself a favor and go outside and make a bonfire, grab some ingredients and a pan, gather round with a few interesting people to discuss the day over a bottle of Nebbiolo, and watch the magic unfold.

Wood-fired cookery is the key to this dish. The smoke of wood embers does something special to fatty sausages and baby turnips cooked in a cast-iron skillet. Hakurei turnips are a mild, sweet, marshmallow-white Japanese variety. They can be enjoyed raw like a radish, pickled, slowly roasted, or grilled. They are much less dense than common purple-type storage turnips, so their cooking time is shorter. Sometimes you can find Hakurei turnips with their greens attached. Cut them off, give them a good clean, and toss them into the pan during the final moments.

A drizzle of sweet vincotto (literally "cooked wine," made by reducing unfermented grape must to a syrup) and a liberal dusting of Parmesan completes the dish. For the sausages, purchase the absolute best you can find, preferably made from a mixture of belly pork and pork shoulder.

4–6 sweet Italian sausages

Olive oil, for cooking

12–14 Hakurei turnips, halved or quartered, depending on size

¼–½ cup water or dry white wine

Pinch of sugar

Kosher salt and freshly ground black pepper

4–5 cloves garlic, thinly sliced

Knob of butter, for finishing

Wedge of Parmesan cheese, for garnish

Vincotto, for drizzling

Bring a large, shallow, wide pot filled with water to a very light simmer. Add the sausages and poach until nearly cooked through and firm, 5–7 minutes. This step can be done up to 3 days in advance; store the sausages in an airtight container in the refrigerator.

Prepare a wood or charcoal fire for cooking over hot embers or coals. Select a cast-iron skillet large enough to hold all the sausages and the turnips. The sausages will be snuggled together but still have a little space on all sides for even cooking and to accommodate the turnips. If your pan isn't large enough, work in batches or use 2 pans. Preheat the skillet over the fire to about 500°F. The pan is ready if when you fling a few drops of cold water onto the bottom, they sizzle and disappear immediately on contact.

Drizzle enough oil into the pan to coat the bottom, plus a little to coat the sausages once they are added. Place the poached sausages in the pan along with the turnips. Pour in the water and add the sugar and a little salt. Cook, turning the sausages as needed to color on all sides, until the water has reduced, the sausages are a glistening golden brown on all sides, and the turnips are tender, 10–12 minutes. Add the garlic during the last couple of minutes and finish with the butter.

Garnish with a storm of grated Parmesan and a drizzle of vincotto and serve with gusto.

HONEY-ROASTED ROOT VEGETABLES

■ **SERVES 4**

The key to roasting any vegetable is using the correct oven temperature. Because of their high water content, less-dense vegetables, such as eggplants, tomatoes, and zucchini, will always need to be roasted in a very hot oven to get a good sear. Denser varieties, such as roots and tubers, which have high starch and low moisture, do best by being shielded from the high heat until tender and then being finished to perfection with a blast of high heat for a final wrinkled crust. In this recipe, the oil, vinegar, and honey play in just the right ways to permeate the skin and caramelize the roots, leaving them almost dessert-like. We love to finish with a contrasting swoosh of honey whipped tahini (page 65), crumbled feta, and a drizzle of salsa verde (page 220).

---

2 lb assorted root vegetables, such as radishes, carrots, turnips, rutabagas, or golden beets

1 large yellow onion

Few fresh thyme or marjoram sprigs

About ⅓ cup olive oil

¼ cup runny honey

Few dashes of sherry vinegar

Kosher salt and freshly ground black pepper

½ lemon (optional)

Torn fresh flat-leaf parsley leaves, for garnish

Crème fraîche, for garnish

Preheat the oven to 400°F. Line a large sheet pan with aluminum foil.

Peel, trim, and cut the root vegetables and onion into manageable pieces all about the same size to ensure even caramelization. Lay them in a single layer on the prepared pan. Add herb sprigs too. Coat them with the oil and then drizzle them with the honey followed by the vinegar. Season liberally and evenly with salt.

Tent the pan with foil and roast the vegetables until fork-tender, about 20 minutes. The timing will depend on the choice of vegetables and the size of the pieces. Remove the foil and roast the vegetables a bit longer until they have a somewhat shrunken appearance and caramel-toned spots.

Remove from the oven, let cool slightly, and then give the vegetables more salt if needed along with a dusting of pepper and perhaps a tiny squeeze of lemon. They should be toasty, nicely salted, and sweet with a bit of tang. Transfer to a nice dish, top with a flourish of parsley and some crème fraîche, and serve right away.

SWEETS
& TREATS

Nothing too sweet, nothing too complicated,
just the right bites to start the day
or close out a fabulous evening.

PALETAS

■ **MAKES ABOUT 8**

Paletas, aka Mexican ice pops, aka the best Popsicles ever! Fresh fruit and bold flavors make these icy treats far better than what the ice cream truck brings by. You can make them tart and refreshing with chunks of fruit and juice or creamy and sweet with condensed milk. Nothing is more enjoyable on a hot summer day, and they can be garnished with everything from shavings of chocolate to chopped nuts to a dusting of chile powder. It's a good idea to always have plenty of frozen goodies on hand that are fun for both kids and adults to eat. I'll take mine upside down in a cup of vodka, please!

---

3 cups chopped fresh fruit

½ cup sugar

⅓ cup filtered water

¼ cup fresh citrus juice of choice

In a blender, combine 1½ cups of the fruit, the sugar, water, and citrus juice and blend until smooth.

Fill ice-pop molds half full with the puréed fruit. Tuck the remaining chopped fruit into the molds, then top with more purée if needed to fill the length, leaving about ½ inch at the top, as the pops will expand as they freeze. If using molds with covers with built-in sticks, cover the molds, slip into the freezer, and freeze until completely frozen, about 4 hours. If using molds that require the addition of a stick, freeze the molds for a couple of hours, add the sticks, and then return to the freezer until frozen solid.

Remove the ice pops from the molds (a very quick dip in warm water will loosen them) and enjoy as is or garnish as you wish. These can be stored in ziplock bags in the freezer for a few weeks.

BERRY BRAN MUFFIN BUCKLES

■ MAKES 12

Nearing the end of my pregnancy, I was going a bit stir-crazy at home getting everything ready for the birth of my son, George. For whatever reason, I was on a mission to make my dream bran muffin come true. Most of the ones you find are as dense as a hockey puck, or taste like a water-soaked bran cereal studded with anemic raisins. I began testing and tweaking to develop a muffin that was light, just sweet enough, and filled with chunks of fresh, juicy fruit. Every day when my husband, John, came home from the farm, I had a version for him to taste, each made with different oils, sweeteners, flours, and fillings.

This recipe is healthy *enough*, and just sweet enough to make you want more. It is a bran muffin so delicious that even the pickiest of children will eat it, and it is tender yet sturdy enough to hold a serious schmear of butter. Fatty nuts and seeds breathe life into the bran base—my favorite combination is pecans and pumpkin seeds—and I change up the fruit depending on where we are in the year. Use any type of fruit within arm's reach. During the warmer months, our farm berries make their way into the mix, while plums, apples, and pears turn up later. Berries that were frozen at the peak of their season are great during the dead of winter, as are dried fruits. Give the nuts or seeds a light toasting before mixing them into the batter; it coaxes out their flavor, giving them a better bite in the muffin. As these muffins cool, the berries will buckle inward and sink into the middle to create the yummiest interior.

Nonstick cooking spray

1 cup whole wheat flour

1 cup wheat germ

1 teaspoon baking soda

1 teaspoon baking powder

1 cup chopped nuts or seeds of choice, lightly toasted

⅓ cup coconut oil, melted and cooled

¼ cup extra-virgin olive oil

¼ cup firmly packed light brown sugar or coconut sugar

1 large egg

1 teaspoon kosher salt

⅓ cup pure maple syrup

¼ cup runny honey

1 cup plain Greek yogurt

1 tablespoon pure vanilla extract

1–2 cups berries or diced fresh or dried fruit of choice

1 cup chopped nuts or seeds of choice, lightly toasted

½ cup raw sugar

Preheat the oven to 400°F. Line 12 standard muffin cups with paper liners and coat them well with nonstick cooking spray.

In a medium bowl, whisk together the flour, wheat germ, baking soda, baking powder, and nuts. In a large bowl, combine the coconut oil, olive oil, brown sugar, egg, and salt and stir to mix well. Add the maple syrup, honey, yogurt, and vanilla and stir again to mix well. Fold the flour mixture into the coconut oil mixture just until the batter is evenly moistened and homogenous.

Spoon the batter into the prepared muffin cups, filling them three-fourths full. Top them with the berries and nuts and then with a generous crumble of raw sugar.

Bake the muffins until they have puffed up and are golden and a toothpick inserted into the center of a muffin comes out mostly clean, about 20 minutes.

Let cool slightly, then remove from the pan and enjoy warm. Leftover muffins can be split, toasted, and served with a giant lump of salty butter.

HOT TIP   The muffin batter can also be baked in a 9 x 5-inch loaf pan. Line the pan with parchment paper and spray the paper with nonstick cooking spray. Spoon the batter into the prepared pan, top with the berries, nuts, and sugar, and bake until the top is golden and a toothpick inserted into the center comes out mostly clean, 35–40 minutes.

BANGIN' BANANA BREAD

■ **MAKES TWO 9 X 5-INCH LOAVES**

No, we do not grow bananas on the farm, and yes, we have been asked that. We do, however, always have rogue bananas lying around the kitchen that we must do something with. I've tinkered with dozens upon dozens of banana bread recipes, and this one is the very best version. The buckwheat and rye flours give it incredible nutty depth. A heavy coat of coarse sugar on top is the pièce de résistance of the whole shebang. The contrast of the crispy sugared exterior against the soft inside is irresistible.

Nonstick cooking spray or unsalted butter, for the pans

2½ cups all-purpose flour

1¼ cups light rye flour

½ cup buckwheat flour

2 tablespoons kosher salt

4 teaspoons baking soda

4 teaspoons baking powder

¼ teaspoon ground cinnamon

⅛ teaspoon ground allspice

⅛ teaspoon freshly grated nutmeg

⅛ teaspoon ground cardamom

1½ cups (12 oz) unsalted butter, melted and cooled

2 cups firmly packed brown sugar

½ cup pure maple syrup

2 lb very ripe bananas, peeled and mashed smooth

4 large eggs

2½ teaspoons pure vanilla extract

Coarse sugar, for topping

Preheat the oven to 325°F. Spray the bottom and sides of two 9 x 5-inch loaf pans with nonstick cooking spray or grease with butter.

In a medium bowl, whisk together the all-purpose flour, rye flour, buckwheat flour, salt, baking soda, baking powder, cinnamon, allspice, nutmeg, and cardamom. In a large bowl, combine the butter, brown sugar, maple syrup, bananas, eggs, and vanilla and stir until smooth. Fold the flour mixture into the butter mixture just until combined and the batter is smooth.

Divide the batter evenly between the prepared pans and sprinkle the tops with a nice layer of coarse sugar. Bake the loaves until a toothpick inserted into the center comes out mostly clean, 45–50 minutes. Let cool completely in the pans on a wire rack.

To keep the crust as crackly as possible, leave the loaves in their pans and do not cover or wrap them. They will keep at room temperature for up to 1 week.

HOT TIPS

If you like, stir 1 cup chocolate chips or lightly toasted and chopped nuts or lightly toasted seeds of choice into the batter just before it goes into the pans.

The loaves can be frozen, but their sugared crust will lose its crunchy luster. When I have a partial leftover loaf, I like to cut it into thick slices and keep them in the freezer so I can pull them out as needed for a breakfast of griddled banana bread French toast.

FRESH BERRIES WITH BROWN SUGAR & WHIPPED CREAM

■ SERVES 4–6

My parents raised me to know good food. Taking me along to dine at fine NYC restaurants, many of which are now shuttered, they showed me the world of my future. They are the reason I cook. Neither of them is a trained chef or even an avant-garde eater, but they love classic flavors, have great taste, and do not succumb to trends. Over the years, they've scoffed at many of my concoctions, but they are also my number-one fans. They've been making this dish ever since I can remember, mostly on humid, warm summer nights in June. It is an elegant dessert that cannot be pegged to time or place and is at its most exceptional when the finest berries are used. I will always think of my parents when I make this perfect, perfectly simple dessert.

3–4 pints fresh berries of choice

2 cups heavy cream (the thickest, richest cream you can find)

1 cup plus 1 tablespoon firmly packed dark brown sugar

Few glugs of pure vanilla extract

Maldon salt, for sprinkling

HOT TIP Making your own vanilla extract is easy! Scoop up a couple of handfuls of plump vanilla beans, split them lengthwise, scrape the seeds into a glass jar or bottle, and throw the pods in behind them. Cover with a couple of cups of light rum, bourbon, or vodka and cap tightly. Store in a dark place for at least 2 to 3 months before using. As the extract gets used, add more alcohol to the jar or bottle to replace it, and let it steep again.

Clean the berries, pat them dry, and place them in a bowl, slicing any large ones into bite-size pieces.

In a bowl, using an electric mixer or a whisk, whip the cream with 1 tablespoon of the sugar and the vanilla until it forms soft peaks.

Get out some fine serving glasses. Go for big-bell red wineglasses for an elegant look or vintage rocks glasses for casual chic. Whatever glasses you choose, make sure you'll be able to see the beautiful layers through them.

Alternately layer the berries and whipped cream in the glasses, sprinkling some brown sugar on top of each berry layer. End with a layer of berries on top, artfully arranging them and hitting them with a twinkle of Maldon salt. Serve within 10 minutes so the brown sugar still offers a little crunchy contrast to the cream.

BUCKWHEAT BLUEBERRY SHORTCAKE

■ MAKES 8 LARGE OR 12 SMALL BISCUITS; SERVES 4–6

A simple dish that can go dramatically wrong if the biscuits are not prepared with care. When executed with the right ingredients and the proper hand, they become magical and quite provocative. Sourcing real pure maple syrup for the berries is an absolute must! Our all-time favorite maple syrup is from Laurel & Ash Farm in the Hudson Valley. It's wood fired, deeply rich in flavor, and truly spectacular. You need to freeze these biscuit babies before baking, so be sure to plan accordingly.

FOR THE BISCUITS

5⅓ cups all-purpose flour or pastry flour, plus more for dusting

1⅔ cups buckwheat flour

1 tablespoon plus 2 teaspoons baking powder

1 tablespoon plus 1 teaspoon kosher salt

1 tablespoon plus 1 teaspoon sugar

Scant ½ teaspoon baking soda

1 lb butter, cut into cubes and kept ice-cold, plus melted butter for brushing

2¼ cups full-fat buttermilk

Maldon salt, for sprinkling

FOR THE BERRIES

3–4 pints berries of choice

½ cup dark maple syrup

Splash of Grand Marnier

1–2 dashes pure vanilla extract

Vanilla whipped cream, for serving

To make the biscuits, in a food processor, combine both flours, the baking powder, kosher salt, sugar, and baking soda, and pulse a few times to mix well. Scatter the butter cubes over the flour mixture and pulse until the mixture forms coarse crumbs. Dump the mixture onto a floured work surface and make a well in the center. Pour the buttermilk into the well, then, using your hands, work the buttermilk into the flour mixture until a loose, ragged dough forms. Cut the dough into thirds, stack the pieces one on top of the other, and roll out the dough 1 inch thick.

Line a large sheet pan with parchment paper. Using a cutter in any shape and size you like, cut out as many biscuits as possible. Arrange them on the prepared sheet pan, spacing them about 1 inch apart. Gather up the dough scraps, press them together, roll out 1 inch thick, cut out more biscuits, and add them to the pan. Wrap the pan in plastic wrap and place it in the freezer until the biscuits are frozen solid, at least 2 hours or up to overnight.

Preheat the oven to 325°F. Unwrap the sheet pan and bake the biscuits from frozen, rotating the pan front to back halfway through baking, until golden brown, about 30 minutes. Remove from the oven and immediately brush the tops with melted butter and finish with a sprinkle of Maldon salt.

While the biscuits are baking, prepare the berries. If using strawberries, hull them and cut them as you like. Leave raspberries, blueberries, or other small berries whole. Put the berries into a bowl, add the maple syrup, Grand Marnier, and vanilla, and toss to mix well.

To serve, cut the warm biscuits in half and place them in individual shallow bowls. Spoon the berries around or over the biscuits and finish each serving with a dollop of whipped cream.

CHOCOLATE BROWNIE TORTE

■ MAKES ONE 8- TO 9-INCH TART

This stellar indulgence is perfectly perfect served all by itself, like a brownie. But if the need arises to dress it up, pair it with no more than a dollop of unsweetened whipped cream and a few raspberries. For a more glam presentation, drape it with a dash of Dark Chocolate Olive Oil Ganache and bits of edible gold leaf. It can be baked in a tart pan and served by the slice or in tartlet pans for personal-size midnight snacks. If well wrapped, it freezes great for a couple of months.

7 oz TCHO dark chocolate (68% cacao) or other high-quality dark chocolate, chopped

14 tablespoons (7 oz) unsalted butter, cut into small chunks

1 cup sugar

4 large eggs

1 tablespoon vanilla bean paste or pure vanilla extract

1 teaspoon kosher salt

3 tablespoons King Arthur gluten-free all-purpose flour (see Hot Tip)

Nonstick cooking spray

FOR THE DARK CHOCOLATE OLIVE OIL GANACHE

1 cup chopped high-quality dark chocolate (about 70% cacao)

2 tablespoons high-quality unsweetened cocoa powder

¼ cup extra-virgin olive oil

1 tablespoon light corn syrup or liquid glucose (to make it shine like a diamond)

Maldon salt

HOT TIP In our opinion, this is the best gluten-free flour on the market, and it means this luscious dessert can be enjoyed by anyone who is gluten sensitive. You can use all-purpose or cake flour in its place.

In a heavy saucepan, combine the chocolate and butter over low heat and heat, stirring often, just until melted and smooth. Remove from the heat and whisk in the sugar, mixing well, then stir for a couple of minutes to cool the mixture down to lukewarm.

Whisk in the eggs, vanilla, and kosher salt, mixing well. Finally, whisk in the flour. Cover the bowl with a kitchen towel or plastic wrap and let sit until the batter thickens, 20–30 minutes.

Preheat the oven to 325°F. Spray the bottom and sides of an 8- to 9-inch tart pan with a removable bottom with nonstick cooking spray. (Alternatively, fill up 2½–inch tartlet plans with removable bottoms and place them on a sheet pan.)

Pour the batter into the prepared pan(s). It should come halfway up the sides. Bake until a toothpick or knife inserted into the center comes out with some fudgy crumbs attached, 20–30 minutes. Let cool on a wire rack for 10 minutes or so before unmolding. The puffed top will sink and crack a bit as the tart cools. Serve warm.

To make the ganache, in a small, heavy saucepan, combine the chocolate, cocoa powder, oil, and corn syrup over medium heat and heat, stirring often, until the chocolate melts and the mixture is smooth and glossy, about 5 minutes. Season to taste with a pinch or two of Maldon salt.

Remove from the heat and pour over the top of a completely cooled cake, making some sexy drips down the sides. Leftover ganache will keep in an airtight container in the refrigerator for a few weeks and can be gently heated to return it to a pourable consistency.

DARKEST CHOCOLATE MOUSSE

■ SERVES 12

Here, our exquisitely lush farm eggs and honey come together in a dreamy dessert guaranteed to impress even the most discerning diner. This mousse is very deeply flavored, rich, and decadent because it is dairy-free. It is much denser than a mousse that contains aerated cream, so if you need to make more than twelve servings for a party, simply shrink the portion size. This recipe is great for entertaining: it benefits from being made in advance, and it can be portioned ahead of time. The eggs are raw, and there is no substitution for them, so you'll want to source the best eggs you can find. If you have stellar chocolate, rich eggs, and quality olive oil, you'll need nothing more than a glass of Champagne or Château d'Yquem to accompany. A small dollop of crème fraîche or vanilla whipped cream alongside is a refreshing contrast, as is a bowl of fresh raspberries or whole cherries over ice.

---

1 lb dark chocolate or blend of dark chocolates, such as TCHO 68% and 99% cacao, chopped

1 cup extra-virgin olive oil, preferably with fruity, buttery notes, plus more for garnish

10 large eggs, chilled

¼ cup runny honey, for the egg yolks

⅓ cup runny honey, for the egg whites

HOT TIP To make this really pop, just before serving, garnish with a drizzle of that fantastic extra-virgin olive oil you splurged on a while back and a few crystals of Maldon salt.

In a heavy saucepan, combine the chocolate and oil over low heat and heat, stirring often, until the chocolate melts and the mixture is smooth. Set aside to cool down a bit.

Have ready 2 medium-size bowls. One at a time, crack the eggs and carefully drop the whites into 1 bowl and the yolks into the other bowl. Add the ¼ cup honey to the egg yolks and, using a handheld electric mixer on medium speed, beat together until the mixture becomes lighter and more buttery in color and doubles in volume, about 10 minutes.

Clean the beaters very, very well so no traces of fatty yolk residue remain. Then, with the mixer on medium speed, beat the egg whites until they become bubbly with a bit of froth.

Take a moment's pause and heat the ⅓ cup honey in a small, heavy pan over medium heat just until it starts to simmer, then remove from the heat. With the mixer on medium speed, stream the simmering honey into the whites, beating them until they form soft peaks. Know that the stiffer you beat your whites, the firmer your mousse will be. Use your best judgment.

Rattle and mix the egg yolks a bit to make sure they haven't lost their character and then gently stir them into the chocolate–olive oil mixture, mixing well until you have a uniform chocolate tone.

Working in a few batches, fold the whipped whites into the chocolate mixture, being as gentle as possible so as not to deflate the whites and folding just until no white swirls are visible in the chocolate.

Pour or spoon the mousse into a larger vessel for portioning later, or spoon it directly into serving glasses or bowls. Cover the surface tightly with plastic wrap to prevent a skin from forming and chill for at least overnight or for up to 1 day.

EXTRA OLIVE OIL CAKE

■ **MAKES ONE 9-INCH CAKE**

In recent years, people in the United States have become more familiar with the use of olive oil in sweets, such as cakes and gelato. Italians, however, have long recognized its versatility in the kitchen and its health benefits. This cake is soaked with olive oil in both flavor and texture. The more intensely flavored the olive oil, the better, and a fruitier oil is preferred over a peppery one. Serve this cake plain alongside an afternoon espresso or dress it up for a luncheon with a dollop of softly whipped cream, sugared blueberries, a bit of citrus zest, and a dash of Maldon salt. And don't forget to finish it all off with a drizzle of more olive oil! This cake can be made in advance—and it should be because it tastes even better the next day.

Butter and all-purpose flour, for the pan

2¾ cups all-purpose flour

2¾ teaspoons kosher salt

1¾ teaspoons baking powder

1 teaspoon baking soda

1½ cups sugar

3 large eggs

1 cup plus 2 tablespoons whole milk

1 cup extra-virgin olive oil, plus more for brushing after baking

½ cup fresh orange juice

1¼ teaspoon grated orange zest

Dash of pure vanilla extract or vanilla bean paste

Preheat the oven to 325°F if using the convection setting or 400°F if using a conventional oven. Generously grease a 9-inch Bundt pan with butter, reaching every nook and cranny, then give it a flour dusting just to be safe, tapping out the excess.

In a medium bowl, whisk together the flour, salt, baking powder, and baking soda. In a large bowl, combine the sugar, eggs, milk, oil, orange juice and zest, and vanilla and stir to mix well. Fold the flour mixture into the oil mixture just until the batter is evenly moistened and homogenous.

Pour the batter into the prepared pan. Bake the cake until a toothpick inserted into the center comes out moderately clean, 45–60 minutes.

Let the cake cool in the pan on a wire rack for 15 minutes. Then brush the top with a good amount of olive oil, unmold the cake onto the rack, lift off the pan, and brush the sides with more oil. Let cool completely before serving.

HONEY BERGAMOT TEA CAKE

■ **MAKES ONE 9-INCH CAKE**

Deeply perfumed with citrus and nutty aromas, this cake is good for any occasion or time of day. It isn't terribly awful for you, nor will it leave you in a listless coma. It pleases those who are gluten-free and those who are dairy-free, making it ideal for nearly any crowd. You can pair it with a cup of tea for breakfast, and it is also enjoyable for dessert. But perhaps it is at its most stellar on a dreary afternoon with a cup of Earl Grey tea and a magazine in hand. Serve with a dollop of clotted cream and a seasonal fruit compote alongside.

Butter and all-purpose flour, for the pan

3 cups blanched almond meal

¼ cup unsweetened shredded dried coconut

¾ teaspoon kosher salt

¾ teaspoon baking powder

Scant ½ teaspoon baking soda

½ cup extra-virgin olive oil

½ cup runny honey

½ teaspoon pure vanilla extract

Few drops of bergamot oil

Grated zest of 2 oranges

⅔ cup fresh orange juice

2 large eggs, whisked

Preheat the oven to 325°F. Grease the sides of a 9-inch springform pan with butter, then dust with flour, tapping out the excess. Line the bottom of the pan with parchment paper and, for extra security, butter and flour the parchment. (If you want this cake to be absolutely gluten-free, use King Arthur gluten-free all-purpose flour or a similar product; to keep it dairy-free, swap out the butter for coconut oil.)

In a large bowl, whisk together the almond meal, coconut, salt, baking powder, and baking soda.

In a small, heavy saucepan, combine the oil and honey over low heat and heat, stirring occasionally, just until the honey liquefies. Remove from the heat and add the vanilla, bergamot oil, and orange zest and juice. Give it a stir.

Add the oil mixture to the almond meal mixture and stir to mix well. Add the eggs and stir until fully incorporated.

Pour the batter into the prepared pan. Bake the cake until a toothpick or knife inserted into the center comes out with just a few crumbs clinging to it, about 1 hour. While the cake bakes, keep the oven light on and don't stray too far. This cake tends to darken quickly. Should the top begin to brown, tent it with aluminum foil to protect it from darkening too much.

Let the cake cool completely in the pan on a wire rack. Then unclasp the pan sides, lift them off, and free the cake from the pan bottom. This cake is the most delicate creature, but if well wrapped, it holds up extremely well in the refrigerator for up to a couple of weeks. And it tastes better when baked a day before serving.

ULTRALUXE PANNA COTTA

■ MAKES TWELVE 4-OZ SERVINGS

Italian for "cooked cream," panna cotta is pure simplicity at its finest. It is an expression of total dairy indulgence, so you must source the very best cream available. Many times, panna cotta is made with too much gelatin, giving it a rubbery texture. This recipe calls for the ideal ratio of rich cream to gelatin, includes the perfect amount of sugar for just a little sweetness, and adds a bit of salt to enhance the overall flavor.

The delicate cream is flavored with a little vanilla, but should you want a slightly different taste profile, you can add some grated citrus zest or a few drops of orange blossom water. Warm spices, such as star anise or grated nutmeg, can be a nice addition once the weather begins to cool. Nearly any fruit—raw, stewed, roasted, or grilled—is a beautiful accompaniment. Or you can go with a more minimalist approach of a drizzle of vincotto or richly aged balsamic vinegar.

Because it calls for a lesser amount of gelatin than most recipes, this panna cotta is a very gentle creature. Handle it with care! It can be poured into separate molds to be delicately inverted onto dessert plates before serving, but it is equally nice served in the ramekins themselves.

---

6 cups heavy cream

¾ cup sugar

1 vanilla bean, split lengthwise, seeds scraped from pod, and pod reserved, or ½ teaspoon vanilla powder or 1 teaspoon vanilla bean paste or pure vanilla extract

¼ teaspoon kosher salt

4 sheets gelatin, or 1 tablespoon powdered gelatin

Get out a very heavy-bottomed pot large enough to hold the cream. Put the cream, sugar, vanilla seeds and pod, and salt into the pot, place over medium-low heat, and stir frequently to dissolve the sugar and keep it from scorching.

Meanwhile, if using gelatin sheets, immerse them in a bowl of ice water for about 5 minutes to soften, then drain and squeeze out the excess water. If using powdered gelatin, put 2 tablespoons of cold water into a small bowl, sprinkle the gelatin on top, stir to combine, then let sit for a few minutes to soften.

Once the cream has begun to simmer, remove the pot from the heat and whisk in the gelatin until fully dissolved.

Fill a large bowl half full with ice cubes and add water just to cover the ice. Pour the hot cream mixture into a bowl, set it over the bowl of ice water, and stir for a few minutes until the temperature drops to lukewarm.

Spoon the mixture into molds or ramekins. If using molds, use ones with smooth sides. The panna cotta is quite fragile, so the less intricacy to the mold, the better. Cover the surface of each one tightly with plastic wrap to prevent a skin from developing and refrigerate for at least 4 hours or up to 1 week.

To unmold, run a paring knife around the inside edge of the mold, invert a plate on top of the mold, invert the mold and plate together, and gently lift off the mold. Top with a drizzle of something luscious or a pile of exquisitely fresh fruit (see headnote).

SALTY BUTTER SPICED GINGERBREAD

■ MAKES ONE 9-INCH BUNDT CAKE

This gingerbread is not for the faint of heart. It is not for those who adore the mild and sweet ginger-bread from a box, and it is definitely not for those who dislike warm spices. It is intense, maybe even spicy to some, and it is boozy, sticky, and very rich. If you like *actual* gingerbread, it's the perfect one for you. It screams the holiday season, and we make it in our household at least once a year. The intensity lends itself to the simplest of accompaniments: a dollop of whipped cream and a smack of powdered sugar. This cake ages gracefully on the countertop or in the refrigerator and is even better after a couple of days—the perfect Bundt for passive holiday snacking.

Butter or nonstick cooking spray and all-purpose flour, for the pan

1 cup Guinness or other dark stout

1 cup blackstrap molasses

½ teaspoon baking soda

2 cups all-purpose flour

1½ teaspoons baking powder

3 tablespoons ground ginger

1 tablespoon ground cinnamon

1 teaspoon ground cloves

1 teaspoon ground allspice

1 teaspoon ground cardamom

½ whole nutmeg, grated

1 teaspoon kosher salt

4–5 twists freshly ground black pepper

3 large eggs

1 cup firmly packed dark brown sugar

1 cup granulated sugar

¾ cup neutral oil, such as canola or grapeseed

1–2 tablespoons pure vanilla extract or vanilla bean paste

½ cup (4 oz) butter, melted

Powdered sugar and whipped cream, for serving

Preheat the oven to 350°F. Generously grease a 9-inch Bundt pan with butter or nonstick cooking spray, reaching every nook and cranny, then dust it with flour, tapping out the excess.

In a saucepan with plenty of room for expansion, combine the Guinness and molasses over medium heat and bring to a gentle simmer, stirring until the molasses liquefies. Remove from the heat, add the baking soda, and watch in glory as all of your seventh-grade science-experiment dreams come true! Give it a stir as it rises and then set aside.

In a medium bowl, whisk together the flour, baking powder, ginger, cinnamon, cloves, allspice, cardamom, nutmeg, salt, and pepper. In a large bowl, vigorously whisk together the eggs, brown sugar, and granulated sugar until the mixture is light in color and airy in texture, about 8 minutes. Whisk in the oil and vanilla, mixing well.

Working in small batches, add the molasses mixture to the egg mixture while whisking constantly. (Adding only a little at a time tempers the egg mixture. Add it too quickly and you'll have scrambled eggs from the heat of the molasses mixture.) Finally, add the flour mixture and stir just until combined.

Pour the batter into the prepared pan. Bake the cake until a knife inserted near the center comes out with just a few moist crumbs clinging to it, 40–50 minutes. Let cool in the pan on a wire rack until it releases a bit from the sides, 3–5 minutes.

With the cake still in the pan, stab every ½ inch or so with a paring knife or thin chopstick. Sop some of the butter all over top and into the holes, either drizzling it or applying it with a pastry brush. Unmold the cake onto the rack, lift off the pan, and brush the sides with the remaining butter.

This cake is best if it has been left to relax on the counter for a day before serving, so go ahead and make it when you have a quiet moment to yourself with a bottle of wine. Then serve it slightly warmed with a dusting of powdered sugar and a mound of whipped cream alongside. Enjoy by a roaring fire.

FRUITY BREAD PUDDING WITH RICH CREAM

■ SERVES 6

Life is like planting an orchard of baby fruit trees: you never know what you're gonna get. In 2022, we set out to plant the foundations of what will be our orchard one day. We sourced offbeat varieties of stone fruits and grapes, all the size of whips, and put them into the ground with much hope. They still have many more years to go. Most fruit trees don't start producing until they are five to seven years old. We have no idea what the fruits will look or taste like when the trees and vines are fully grown—or if they will ever even have fruit! Until that fine day when we can use our own fruit, we buy the best we can find from farms throughout the Hudson Valley that have been around since long before us.

FOR THE FRUIT

8–12 fresh apricots, plums, peaches, or nectarines, pitted and cut into chunks; 2 cups pitted fresh cherries; or 1–2 cups dried stone fruits

1½ cups granulated sugar

Pinch of kosher salt

FOR THE PUDDING

1 lb day-old brioche or sourdough bread

8 large egg yolks

½ cup granulated sugar

3 cups heavy cream

1 cup whole milk

Splash of brandy or kirsch

Grated zest of 1 orange

1 teaspoon kosher salt

1–2 tablespoons pure vanilla extract or vanilla bean paste

Tiny dash of pure almond extract

Dusting of freshly grated nutmeg

2 grates from a cinnamon stick

3–4 tablespoons almond paste (optional)

4 tablespoons (2 oz) butter

Coarse sugar and Maldon salt, for topping

Vanilla ice cream or heavy cream and sliced almonds (optional), for serving

To prepare the fruit, in a saucepan, combine the fruit, a few tablespoons of the granulated sugar, the kosher salt, and about 1 scant cup water over medium heat, bring to a gentle simmer, and poach until the fruit is tender, 10–15 minutes for fresh fruit and longer for dried. Remove from the heat and, using a slotted spoon, transfer the fruit to a bowl to cool.

Return the pan to the stove top over medium heat. Add the remaining granulated sugar and a little more water and reduce the liquid to a brownish caramel-like sticky state, about 8 minutes. Pour the hot caramel sauce into the bottom of a 2-quart baking dish or divide evenly among 6 ramekins.

Preheat the oven to 375°F. Line a sheet pan with aluminum foil.

To make the pudding, cut off the crusts from the bread, cut the bread into ½-inch cubes, and set aside. In a large bowl, whisk together the egg yolks and granulated sugar until well mixed, then whisk in the cream, milk, and brandy until fully incorporated. Add the orange zest, kosher salt, vanilla, almond extract, nutmeg, and cinnamon and whisk well. Gently fold in the cooled fruit and the bread until evenly distributed.

Spoon the pudding mixture into the caramel-lined baking dish or divide evenly among the ramekins. Break the almond paste (if using) into small crumbs and cut the butter into bits, then tuck all the pieces into the pudding mixture, spacing them evenly around the dish. Coat the top with a nice amount of coarse sugar and finish with a little Maldon salt. Place the baking dish or ramekins on the prepared sheet pan and bake the pudding until nicely browned on top, about 1 hour.

Serve warm or at room temperature. If serving warm, accompany with a scoop of top-notch ice cream or an ample pour of heavy cream and a final sprinkle of Maldon salt. You can also add a scattering of almonds if you like. The pudding can be made a few days in advance, covered, and refrigerated and then reheated in a 250°F oven before serving.

THE ALMIGHTY EGG

Most everything you source from local farms will have far better taste than their commodity equivalents, but the difference for some products will be more significant than others. Eggs are at the top of the heap. Experiencing eggs from well-cared-for, healthy chickens that have been allowed to roam freely and to eat lots of bugs and foods that span the colors of the rainbow will change a person's thoughts on what an egg is. Sadly, though, very few people in the United States get to enjoy this type of rich butt nugget due to poor practice standards, increasing demand, the cost of producing true free-range eggs, and the perceived market value.

The consumer understanding of what goes into small-farm egg production is very limited, which makes mass-produced eggs far more common in most household refrigerators. They are often disguised by fancy packaging displaying misleading phrases like "free range" and "vegetarian raised," causing the consumer to believe the young ladies who laid these eggs are meant to be vegetarian, when that couldn't be further from the truth. Inside the cartons are anemic shells filled with pale yolks and runny whites, which is proof of the lack of nutrition and the unnatural conditions the hens were subjected to. Given the opportunity to roam in a natural environment, chickens adore eating bugs of all kinds, especially ticks, and frogs too! They eat meat and enjoy deer carcasses to nibble on during the depth of winter. They've even been known to consume their own eggs and each other!

Chickens are indispensable to any animal rotation on a farm and help with both soil health and pest maintenance when allowed to roam freely. When not given enough space, they will destroy the ground, leaving the earth barren and bleak. On the farm, we rotate them regularly to fresh parcels of pasture. We save diverse scraps of food from going to compost and give them to our little winged friends instead. They love to peck, nibble, and enjoy everything from cheese rinds to the hottest of peppers (fun fact: chickens don't have taste buds to sense heat). Truth be told, they are baby dinosaurs that will even pluck flies and grain out from the messiest of cow pies!

Because of this diverse diet and vast environment, our chickens produce the most glorious eggs, with deep golden-orange yolks, tight whites, and thick, strong shells. They are far richer than any mass-produced egg you will eat, which makes it nearly impossible to eat as many.

Eggs that have been produced with care on small farms will absolutely carry a higher cost—and be worth it! (Industrial farming has skewed people's idea of the cost of all food items but especially eggs.) We find the eggs from our little hens to be one of the most valuable luxuries on our farm. They are rich, delicious works of art and are seasonal, just like our precious produce. They deserve to be handled with respect.

Egg dishes, when executed correctly, radiate an air of elegance. They have an allure, grandeur, and swagger that sets them apart from any other ingredient-specific cookery. When mishandled, however, they are typically rubbery, under-seasoned, overcooked, and virtually unrecognizable from their true potential. Once you've mastered how to cook them well, eggs become meditative in prepa-ration and a delight to serve to others. They can be dressed up with fresh butter, caviar, and truffles or humbly cooked for just minutes in boiling water and served alongside toast points—very different preparations but both great. Eggs elevate dishes, literally and figuratively. They bind ingredients as well as tenderize. They make for the creamiest of pastry fillings, are packed with protein and healthy fats, and are spatially efficient. They even make for a great hair mask!

Egg cookery is common to all countries and boasts thousands of variations, from hard-to-master soufflés to much simpler soft scrambles made on a quiet morning at home. No matter how eggs are prepared, there is no greater satisfaction than an egg dish done right with great eggs.

Note: In the United States and some other countries, eggs are washed and refrig-erated in order to be sold, which actually shortens their shelf life. But washing is not necessary—and most of the world does not do it. Left unwashed, with their natural antibacterial coating intact, eggs will last for a couple of months on a kitchen counter.

ZABAGLIONE

■ SERVES 12

I consider zabaglione, or sabayon in French, the Coco Chanel of desserts: sophisticated, graceful, and timeless—it goes great with everything. This most soothing concoction is made from just three humble ingredients—eggs, wine, and sugar—which are transformed into a wine-scented cloudlike froth that is one of the most ethereal textures known to man.

While the ingredients list is simple, the equipment really, really matters. Zabaglione can be made over an open flame, though I would not recommend it unless you have a traditional round-bottomed copper bowl and a master's degree in heat control. A double boiler is a safer, more practical choice. The ingredients are ideally whipped up in an unlined copper bowl, but a heatproof glass bowl is the next-best option. It offers more even heat distribution than stainless steel or ceramic. Always use a larger bowl than you think you will need. The egg yolks increase dramatically in volume over the heat, and you want to make sure you don't overflow the sides of the bowl into the flames below. The water pot should be large enough to accommodate the bottom and about halfway up the sides of the bowl. The two vessels should have a nice snug fit when nested together, and the water that is simmering in the pot should be about an inch below the bottom of the bowl. Last but not least, have a sturdy whisk that can take a beating, preferably a balloon type. A handheld electric mixer with a whisk attachment will also suffice for lazy days. For a smaller gathering, this recipe can be cut exactly in half to serve six.

---

8 sumptuous and vibrant large egg yolks

½ cup sugar

1 cup dry Marsala wine

Pinch of kosher salt

Pinch of seeds scraped from a vanilla bean, or dash of fresh lemon juice (optional)

Fruit, biscotti or amaretti, or plain cake, for serving

HOT TIP I love baking off a couple of sugar-coated sheets of puff pastry to break into shards for a striking garnish.

VARIATION For a deeper-flavored version, substitute a big, juicy red wine, such as a Barbaresco or Valpolicella, for the Marsala. But keep in mind that this version is better served cold. Make it in the same way as the Marsala version, but chill it for 4–8 hours before serving.

Place the yolks and sugar in a heatproof bowl—one that is large enough and will eventually make its way onto a pot as part of a double boiler. You need to mix the eggs and sugar together immediately, as the sugar will burn the yolks and create lumps if they sit for a moment too long. Using a whisk and a strong arm or a handheld electric mixer on medium speed, whip together the yolks and sugar until pale yellow and creamy.

Pour water into the pot to a depth of 4–6 inches and bring to a fast simmer. Make sure it is not at a boil. Fit the bowl of eggs and sugar on top of the pot over (but not touching) the simmering water. While beating constantly, begin to add the Marsala along with the salt to coax the flavors out. This is not the time to catch up on text messages or let the dog out. Keep your hand whipping, stand up straight, and focus!

Once all the Marsala is in the bowl, the mixture will begin to get a tad foamy and then it will start to grow in size, becoming a light, frothy mass. Keep going until it begins to thicken. It is ready when it forms soft mounds, which is usually after about 15 minutes of whipping. Whip in the vanilla seeds if you like and remove from the heat.

The zabaglione is most amazing when served slightly warm or at room temperature, but it can also be chilled and served cold. Spoon it into your fanciest coupes or cutest bowls and serve with fresh berries or other fruits, biscotti or amaretti, or alongside a very plain cake.

SUMMER PUDDING

■ SERVES 4–6

A popular old-school English dessert, this pudding is a wonderful expression of the essence of summer. Slices of stale bread and rogue berries are transformed into a vibrantly hued, juicy dome that can be made a day ahead to ensure an impressive, low-stress party dessert. Any mix of berries will be good here, as will just one type. For the bread, we love to use shokupan (Japanese milk bread), but any dense, enriched white sandwich bread will work. Topping each serving tableside with a drizzle of heavy cream is lovely, but depending on how good your berries are, you may find that this classic dessert is more delicious with no cream at all.

2 lb fresh berries, stemmed if needed (about 6 cups)

½ cup sugar, or more, depending on your berries and sweet tooth

Pinch of kosher salt

Few drops of pure vanilla extract, or few pinches of grated citrus zest (optional)

1-lb loaf day-old dense white sandwich bread, cut into slices about ½ inch thick

Heavy cream, for serving

In a saucepan, combine the berries, sugar, and salt over medium heat and cook gently for a few minutes until the berries have softened. Remove from the heat, stir in the vanilla (if using), and let cool.

Trim off the crusts from the bread slices. Select a 2-quart bowl or round dish, such as a soufflé dish. Line the bowl with the bread slices, trimming them to fit as needed. The dish must be completely lined, bottom and sides, with positively no gaps for the juice to escape. Double up on areas if necessary.

Fill the bread-lined bowl with the berry mixture, reserving about half of the juice in the bottom of the pan for the final presentation. Top the fruit with a layer of bread slices, again leaving no gaps.

Cover the bowl with plastic wrap. Select a plate that will just fit inside the rim of the bowl, or cut out a cardboard round to fit. Place the plate or cardboard round on the pudding, then top with a weight, such as a cast-iron pan or a stack of bowls. This will press the pudding down, giving the berries and bread a chance to become one. Slip the weighted pudding and the reserved berry juice into the refrigerator and leave overnight.

When ready to serve the pudding, remove the weight, plate, and plastic wrap. Invert a shallow serving dish (juice will overflow the sides of a completely flat one) over the bowl, invert the dish and bowl together, and lift off the bowl. Pour the reserved berry juice over the pudding, then slice into portions, plate them, and top each one with a drizzle of thick, fresh cream.

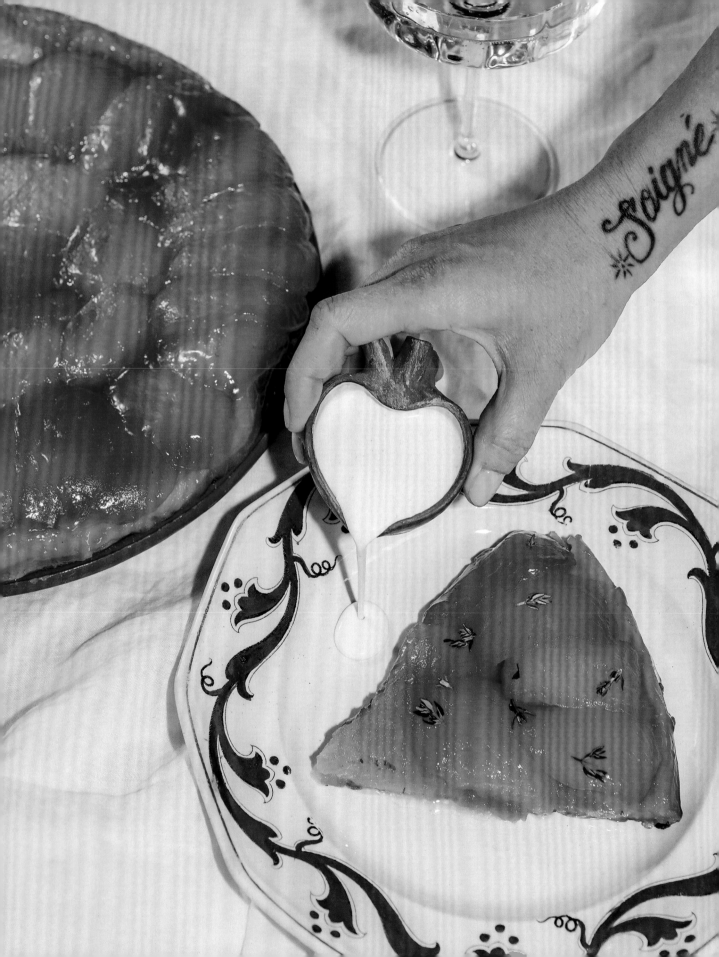

TARTE TATIN

- **SERVES 6–10**

Just because I *can* make pie dough doesn't mean I like to or even want to. That's why I always have a pack or two of puff pastry dough in my freezer for those occasions when I need to pull off a dessert reminiscent of pie. I find tarte Tatin to be much tastier and, honestly, more impressive than humble pie. It is juicy, tangy, rich, and simpler to make than any pie I've come across. Using very tart apples, or even a mix of apples and pears, helps to combat the sweetness of the caramelized sugar, making the tarte pleasantly balanced. Serve it slightly warm with a drizzle of heavy cream and a few thyme leaves, or with a spoonful of rich vanilla ice cream alongside. A glass of Champagne pairs nicely.

About 8 or so firm, tart, non-mealy apples, such as Ginger Gold or Honeycrisp

½ cup (4 oz) butter, at room temperature

2 pinches of kosher salt

Scant 1 cup granulated sugar, firmly packed light brown sugar, or coconut sugar

1 lemon, halved

All-purpose flour, for dusting

1 sheet puff pastry (such as Dufour brand), about 10 oz, thawed according to package instructions (see Hot Tips)

2 tablespoons apricot jam mixed with a bold splash of brandy

Maldon salt, for finishing

HOT TIPS

Several commercial puff pastry doughs contain a lot of preservatives and other additives, so make sure you read the label before you buy. Try to stay away from brands that list much more than butter, flour, and salt.

If you make this tart a couple of days before serving, refrigerate it in the pan, then warm it a little in a 350°F oven before inverting to serve.

Peel, core, and quarter the apples through the stem end. Keep a half of one of the apples whole to serve as the center apple around which you will place the apple quarters. The apples can be peeled and cut a day or two in advance and stored in an airtight container in the refrigerator. Some say it's even better to cut them in advance because it gives them a chance to dry out a little. They will turn brown when cooked, so don't bother adding any water or acid to help them keep their color.

Preheat the oven to 375°F. Get out a 12-inch cast-iron skillet and coat the bottom with the butter. Sprinkle the kosher salt over the butter followed by the sugar, then shake the pan to spread the sugar out evenly over the bottom.

Place the reserved apple half in the center of the pan. Arrange the apple quarters around the apple half in concentric circles, standing them on their flat side and placing them close together. Squeeze some lemon juice over the apples to impart a little brightness as they cook.

On a lightly floured work surface, roll out the puff pastry to about ¼ inch thick. Using an inverted bowl the diameter of your skillet as your guide, cut out a circular shape to fit over the skillet. Drape the dough round over the apples in the pan, tucking in any runaway sides and hugging the apples together with the pastry.

Place the skillet over medium heat until it steams and the juices bubbling around the edges of the pan turn a deep golden brown, 10–12 minutes. Transfer the pan to the oven and bake until the puff pastry is golden and crisp, about 40 minutes.

Let cool for 10 minutes, then carefully invert onto a dish or platter that has a bit of a side to catch the syrupy juice. Should you lose any apples, that's OK! This is a forgiving dish. Just tuck them back in where they belong and go about your day. Brush the top with the brandy–apricot jam mixture and finish with a few crystals of Maldon salt. Serve warm but not hot.

THE BEST CARROT CAKE

- **SERVES 10–12**

We love having our produce stand out in any dish, including cake, which is why you will find kick-ass strands of carrot in this recipe. The addition of brown butter to nearly anything, but especially to this frosting, imparts a nutty, rich flavor that we can't get enough of. This cake benefits from being frosted the day before serving so the frosting and cake can meld together, rather than just sit next to each other. People who have had this dessert swear it is the best carrot cake they've ever eaten, which is why we gave it this name. We'd be lying if we didn't think it's due to our carrots.

FOR THE CAKE

Nonstick cooking spray, for the pan

1¼ cups all-purpose flour

¼ cup whole wheat flour

1 teaspoon kosher salt

¾ teaspoon baking powder

¾ teaspoon baking soda

2 cups unsweetened shredded dried coconut

3 large eggs

¾ cup granulated sugar

¼ cup firmly packed dark brown sugar

1 cup neutral oil, such as canola or grapeseed

1 tablespoon pure vanilla extract or vanilla bean paste

½ lb or so amazing farmers' market carrots, grated

½ cup apricot jam

FOR THE FROSTING

1 lb butter

1 lb cream cheese, at room temperature

1–2 tablespoons pure vanilla extract or vanilla bean paste

2 generous pinches of kosher salt

1 lb powdered sugar

To make the cake, preheat the oven to 325°F. Spray the bottom and sides of two 8-inch round cake pans or 1 half sheet pan (18 by 13 by 1 inch) with nonstick cooking spray, then line the bottom with parchment paper.

In a medium bowl, whisk together both flours, the salt, baking powder, baking soda, and coconut. In a stand mixer fitted with the whip attachment, combine the eggs, granulated sugar, and brown sugar and beat on medium speed until doubled in volume, about 6 minutes. Add the oil and vanilla and continue to beat for another 6 minutes or so. The mixture will begin to lose volume. That means you're on the right track! On low speed, add the flour mixture and beat just until combined. Using a rubber spatula, gently fold in the carrots and jam just until evenly distributed. Do not overmix.

Pour the batter into the prepared pan(s). Bake the cake until a toothpick inserted into the center comes out clean, 20–30 minutes. The timing will depend on the depth of the pan. Let cool completely in the pan(s) on a wire rack, then turn out onto the rack and peel away the parchment.

While the cake is baking, make the frosting. In a sauté pan, melt the butter over medium heat. At first, the butter will foam and then the milk solids will begin to brown at the bottom of the pan. Continue to heat, stirring occasionally, until the milk solids turn a deep chocolate brown and the butter smells nutty, then remove from the heat and let cool. In the stand mixer fitted with the whip attachment, cream together the cooled brown butter and cream cheese on medium speed until thoroughly blended and smooth, then beat in the vanilla and salt. On medium-low speed, add the powdered sugar in two or three batches, beating after each addition until incorporated, then continue to beat on medium speed until fluffy.

To assemble a layer cake, stack the 8-inch cake rounds or cut the sheet-pan cake crosswise into thirds and stack the pieces. Spread frosting between the layers and on the top and sides. Or if you are not feeling fancy and want to get at the cake snack-style, just frost it in a single layer.

OTHER USEFUL TIDBITS

Baby basics that will make your
life a whole lot tastier.

SAUCES, DIPS & MORE

The beauty of simple sauces and dips, particularly ones containing an abundance of herbs, is that you can adjust them as needed with what you have on hand. Raw, herbaceous, and vibrant, sauces come in an array of guises and can elevate and complement the simplest of cookery. Always use the freshest, most fragrant ingredients you can source for your sauces, as only then will their flavors and the flavor of what they grace truly shine.

———

Raw Tomatillo Salsa Verde
Makes about 3 cups

1 lb or so tomatillos, husks removed, rinsed, and quartered
2–4 cloves garlic
½ cup roughly chopped white onion
1–2 fresh green chiles, such as jalapeño or serrano, roughly chopped
Juice of 1–2 limes
Kosher salt
⅔ cup fresh cilantro leaves and stems, roughly chopped
Pinch of ground cumin (optional)

In a food processor, combine the tomatillos, garlic, onion, chiles, lime juice, and a hefty pinch of salt, pulse a few times to move stuff around, and then process until you have a thick purée. Add the cilantro and the cumin (if using) and pulse until the cilantro is evenly mixed and visible as flecks. Taste and adjust with salt if needed. Serve the salsa right away or transfer to an airtight container and let sit in the refrigerator for a few hours before serving.

———

Herby Salsa Verde
Makes a generous 2 cups

2 cups roughly chopped fresh basil, mint, cilantro, flat-leaf parsley, and green onion, in any combination
¼ cup capers
2–4 cloves garlic, finely chopped or thinly sliced
1–2 shallots, minced
1 Fresno or other fresh green chile, roughly chopped or sliced, or pinch of red chile flakes
Few small splashes of sherry vinegar or red wine vinegar

Grated zest and juice of 1–2 lemons (orange is also great)
Freshly ground black pepper
1½ cups buttery extra-virgin olive oil, plus more for topping if needed
2–3 teaspoons kosher salt

In a bowl, combine the herbs, capers, garlic, shallots, chile, vinegar, lemon zest and juice, a few twists of pepper, and the oil and stir gently to mix. Season with 2 teaspoons of the salt, then give the mixture another stir and let sit for 20 minutes or so on the counter.

Taste and adjust with a little more salt and/or acid until the sauce tastes herbaceous and ultra fresh. Use immediately, or transfer to an airtight container. If the herbs are not completely submerged, top with a little oil to prevent oxidation. The sauce will keep in the refrigerator for a couple of weeks or in the freezer for up to 3 months.

———

Mojo Verde
Makes a scant 2 cups

2 cups fresh cilantro leaves and stems
2–3 cloves garlic
1–2 green or yellow chiles, roughly chopped
1 teaspoon cumin seeds, toasted and crushed
2–3 splashes of aged sherry vinegar
2–3 squeezes of fresh orange juice
1–2 drops of runny honey or agave nectar
2 generous pinches of kosher salt
½–1 cup extra-virgin olive oil

In a food processor, combine the cilantro, garlic, chiles, and cumin and blitz to break them up. Add the vinegar, orange juice, honey, and salt and pulse once or twice to mix. Then, with the processor running, drizzle in enough oil to achieve the desired consistency. You can leave it a bit chunky or process it until smooth. Taste and adjust the seasoning with honey, acids, and salt to find a nice balance. Use immediately, or transfer to an airtight container, top with a little oil to prevent oxidation, cap tightly, and store in the refrigerator for up to 1 week.

Ají Verde
Makes about 4 cups

½ cup thick mayonnaise, such as Hellmann's
or Best Foods

¼ cup extra-virgin olive oil

About 1 cup crumbled or grated cheese,
such as queso fresco or Parmesan (about ¼ lb)

3–4 cloves garlic

2 fresh green chiles, chopped (we like serranos)

1 cup or so roughly chopped fresh cilantro leaves and stems

1 cup or so roughly chopped fresh Mexican mint marigold
leaves and flowers

3–4 tablespoons chopped shallot or green onion

Juice of 2–3 limes, plus 1–2 pinches of grated zest

½–1 tablespoon ají amarillo paste (optional)

Few generous pinches of kosher salt

1–2 drops of agave nectar or runny honey

In a food processor, combine all the ingredients and
process until completely smooth. Taste and adjust
as needed with lime, ají amarillo paste (if using), salt,
and agave nectar. Use immediately, or transfer to an
airtight container and store in the refrigerator for up
to 1 week.

Spring Pistou
Makes about 1 cup

1–3 cloves garlic

Kosher salt

4–5 cups fresh greens of choice, such as ramp tops, basil,
flat-leaf parsley, or petite kale or Swiss chard leaves, torn
into small pieces

½ cup extra-virgin olive oil, plus more as needed

1–2 pinches of minced green chile or freshly ground
black pepper

Pinch of grated lemon zest (optional)

If using a mortar and pestle, put the garlic and a
generous pinch of salt in the mortar and grind to
a paste. Add the greens, little by little, and grind
until they start to become smooth, drizzling in the
oil along the way. Once all the greens have been
incorporated, add more oil if the sauce seems too
thick. If using a food processor or blender, combine
the garlic and a generous pinch of salt and pulse a
few times to break down the garlic. Add the greens
and oil and blitz until you have a good consistency,
adjusting with more oil as needed.

Stir in the chile and lemon zest (if using), then taste
and adjust with salt if needed. Use immediately, or
transfer to an airtight container, top with a little oil
to prevent oxidation, cap tightly, and store in the
refrigerator for up to 2 weeks.

Note: The blades of a food processor or blender
cause a lot of friction, friction causes heat, and heat
can cause the greens to oxidize to a hue similar to
that of parrot shit. To prevent this from happening,
or to ensure a vivid green, briefly blanch the greens
in boiling water, then shock in ice water and pat dry
before processing or blending.

If you want to include a nut for a richer taste, toasted
pine nuts are a good choice.

Late-Summer Pesto
Makes a generous 2 cups

2–4 cloves garlic
2 pinches of kosher salt
1 cup mild extra-virgin olive oil, plus more as needed
1/3 cup toasted nuts or seeds, such as pine nuts, walnuts, sunflower or pumpkin seeds, or a combination
2–3 cups fresh herbs or greens of choice, such as basil, watercress, or arugula
3/4 cup grated hard cheese, such as Parmesan, grana, pecorino, Manchego, or aged Gouda or a combination
Grated lemon zest, for seasoning (optional)
Pinch of red chile flakes (optional)

In a food processor, combine the garlic, salt, and a splash of oil and blitz until the garlic is broken down. Add the nuts and blitz again with a tad more oil until a chunky paste forms. Add the herbs and the rest of the oil and blitz until the desired texture is reached. Stir in the cheese with a rubber spatula and then stir in a little more oil if needed for a good consistency. Taste and season with the lemon zest and chile flakes if you like and a bit more salt if needed. Use immediately, or transfer to an airtight container, top with a little oil to prevent oxidation, cap tightly, and store in the refrigerator for up to 2 weeks.

—

Wintry Pistachio Pesto
Makes about 4 cups

1 cup extra-virgin olive oil, plus more for topping
1/2 cup chopped garlic
2 cups fresh sage leaves
2 cups unsalted pistachios, lightly toasted
2 cups fresh flat-leaf parsley leaves
Grated zest and juice of 6 lemons
Grated zest of 1 orange
2 pinches of red chile flakes or cayenne pepper
Kosher salt

In a small saucepan, combine the oil and garlic over medium heat and bring to a gentle simmer, adjusting the heat as needed, until the garlic pieces caramelize to a light golden brown, 3–4 minutes. Do not let the garlic burn! Lightly caramelizing the garlic gives it a nice toasty, deep flavor. Remove from the heat and add the sage, immersing the leaves completely in the oil. Let cool completely.

In a food processor, combine the pistachios, parsley, lemon and orange zests, chile flakes, and about 2 teaspoons salt and blitz until a coarse paste forms. Add the cooled oil and sage and the lemon juice and process until chunky or the desired texture. Give the sauce a taste and adjust with salt as needed.

To keep the lush green color, immediately transfer to airtight containers, top with a little oil to prevent oxidation, cap tightly, and refrigerate for up to 1 month or freeze for up to 3 months.

Note: For a silky-smooth pesto, transfer the finished pesto to a blender and blitz on high speed until creamy. You may need to add a little water or a drizzle of oil to thin it out a bit, and depending on the strength of your blender, you may want to work in batches.

—

Habanada Pesto
Makes 3–4 cups

1 cup Marcona almonds
4–6 cloves garlic, smashed
14–16 Habanada peppers, stemmed and then seared in a cast-iron pan over high heat to soften
Splash of mild vinegar or fresh lemon juice, plus more as needed
Kosher salt
1 can (14 1/2 oz) San Marzano tomatoes, with their juices
2–3 handfuls of fresh basil leaves
12 or so fresh mint leaves
1/2 cup extra-virgin olive oil, plus more if needed
About 6 oz Parmesan and/or mild pecorino cheese, grated
Pinch of red chile flakes or finely chopped fresh red chile

In a blender, combine the almonds, garlic, Habanada peppers, vinegar, and a pinch of salt and pulse until a chunky purée forms. Add the tomatoes, basil, mint, and oil and pulse again until incorporated but even chunkier. Finally, add the cheese and chile flakes and pulse to incorporate, then add more oil or vinegar if needed for bright flavor and a smoother texture. Use immediately, or transfer to an airtight container, top with a little oil to prevent oxidation, cap tightly, and store in the refrigerator for up to 2 weeks.

Poblano Green Goddess Dressing

Makes a generous 2 cups

1–2 poblano chiles, roasted, peeled, and seeded

1 jalapeño chile, roasted, peeled, and seeded (optional)

½ cup chopped fresh cilantro, pipicha, or papalo

½ cup pepitas, toasted to dark golden

⅓ cup chopped green onions, white and green parts

1 robust clove garlic, grated

Grated zest and juice of 3–4 limes

1 cup full-fat buttermilk

¼ cup extra-virgin olive oil

1–2 tablespoons agave nectar

Pinch of toasted cumin seeds

Kosher salt

In a blender or food processor, combine the poblano chile, jalapeño chile (if using), cilantro, pepitas, green onions, garlic, lime zest and juice, buttermilk, oil, agave nectar, and cumin and purée until smooth and pourable, adding water if needed to thin. Season with salt. Use immediately or refrigerate for up to 1 week.

—

Miso-Maple-Tahini Dressing

Makes a generous 2 cups

¼ cup pure dark maple syrup

¼ cup high-quality tahini, such as Soom brand, well stirred until smooth

⅓ cup aged sherry vinegar

¼ cup extra-virgin olive oil

Juice of 1–2 lemons

1–2 tablespoons barley miso or robust darker style of miso

Pinch of cayenne pepper

Kosher salt

In a bowl, whisk together the maple syrup, tahini, vinegar, oil, lemon juice, and miso until creamy and emulsified. (Or process in a blender.) Add the cayenne, season with salt, and stir well. This dressing will thicken up quite a bit as it sits, so thin with water as needed before using. It will keep refrigerated for up to 1 week.

The Best Blue Cheese Dressing

Makes about 2½ cups

½ cup sour cream, crème fraîche, or labne

½ cup mayonnaise

½ cup full-fat buttermilk, plus more as needed

¼ lb Gorgonzola dolce cheese, crumbled

¼ cup extra-virgin olive oil

1 small shallot, minced

1 clove garlic, grated

Juice of 1–2 lemons

Pinch of grated lemon zest

2 dashes of hot sauce, such as Crystal or Tabasco

⅓ cup crumbled piquant blue cheese, such as Stilton

1–2 tablespoons minced fresh flat-leaf parsley

1–2 tablespoons minced fresh chives

Kosher salt and freshly ground black pepper

In a food processor, combine the sour cream, mayonnaise, buttermilk, Gorgonzola, oil, shallot, garlic, lemon juice and zest, and hot sauce and process until smooth. Adjust the thickness with water, lemon juice, or buttermilk if needed for a good consistency. Transfer to a bowl, stir in the piquant blue cheese, parsley, chives, a pinch of salt, and a few cracks of pepper, then taste and adjust the seasoning if needed. Cover and refrigerate overnight before using. It will keep for up to 1 week.

—

Fancy Ranch Dressing

Makes about 2 cups

½ cup Kewpie mayonnaise

½ cup crème fraîche or labne

1 clove garlic, grated

Juice of 1–2 lemons

1 drop of agave nectar

½ cup full-fat buttermilk, more or less

½ cup minced fresh herb, such as dill, flat-leaf parsley, or chives

Kosher salt

In a bowl, whisk together the mayonnaise, crème fraîche, garlic, lemon juice, and agave nectar. Whisk in the buttermilk, adding more for a thinner consistency or less for a thicker one. Fold in the herb and season with salt. Cover and refrigerate for at least a few hours or up to overnight. Taste and adjust with salt if needed before using.

Marcella's Tomato Sauce

Makes about 4 cups

One of my all-time favorites, this famous tomato sauce was written by Marcella Hazan, the godmother of Italian cooking. Foolproof and perfectly balanced, this recipe is about to change your world for the better.

2 (28-oz) cans San Marzano tomatoes, with juice
½–¾ cup (6–8 oz) butter, cut into pieces
1–2 yellow onions, halved
Kosher salt
A few fresh basil leaves (optional)

In a saucepan, combine the tomatoes and their juice, butter, and onions and simmer gently over low heat, stirring occasionally and mashing up the tomatoes as they soften, until the sauce is slightly thickened, 45 minutes to 1 hour. You can discard the onions—Marcella did—or break them up into the sauce. Season with salt and stir in the basil (if using).

Basic Chicken Stock

Makes 5–6 quarts

4 lb chicken wings
Handful of chicken feet
8 quarts water
2 carrots, halved
1 large yellow onion, quartered
2 celery ribs, halved
1 leek, white and green parts, halved
1 head garlic, halved (optional)
3–4 bay leaves
Fistful of fresh flat-leaf parsley
Several fresh thyme sprigs
1–2 tablespoons black peppercorns
Kosher salt

In a large pot, combine the chicken wings and feet and the water and bring to a boil over high heat. Turn down the heat to a bare simmer and skim off the foam and scuzz that rises to the top, leaving any fat behind (it will add flavor throughout the cooking). Add the carrots, onion, celery, leek, garlic (if using), bay leaves, parsley, thyme, and peppercorns and simmer for 1–4 hours. The longer you simmer, the more the stock will reduce and the more concentrated the flavor will be. Remove from the heat and season with salt. Let cool, strain through a fine-mesh sieve, and discard all the solids. For a more refined stock, line the sieve with a large coffee filter or cheesecloth and strain again. Pour into small containers for freezing for up to 3 months or store in larger containers in the refrigerator for up to 1 week.

PICKLES & PRESERVES

Pickled and preserved foods can range from the most piquant and savory to the sweetest of sweet. They can complement everything from breakfast to a casual picnic to a charcuterie board and can be the pièce de résistance that sets off a main or dessert. All of them are easy to make once you master the method, and I have found they are an indispensable item in my refrigerator, freezer, and pantry and on my kitchen table. The honey pickle brine here can be poured over any vegetable and is delicious.

—

Honey Pickles
Makes about 2 quarts pickling liquid

5 cups rice vinegar
2 cups water
1½ cups runny honey or pure maple syrup
4–5 tablespoons kosher salt
Vegetable of choice, for pickling

In a heavy saucepan, combine the vinegar, water, honey, and salt over medium heat and bring to a simmer, stirring to dissolve the honey and salt. Remove from the heat and let cool for about 5 minutes until moderately warm. Then pour over the vegetable you're pickling and let cool completely.

For a deeper honey flavor: Caramelizing the honey in the pan before adding the liquid will yield a deeper flavor. Put the honey into the pan, add a spoonful or two of the water, and heat over low heat, stirring often. Once the honey begins to bubble, stop stirring and let it cook for a couple of minutes until the color deepens and the aroma turns nutty. Then add the remaining ingredients and proceed as directed.

Pickled Baby Ginger
Makes about 2 cups

1 lb baby ginger
1 cup rice vinegar
½ cup filtered water
½ cup runny honey or sugar
About 3 tablespoons kosher salt
Aromatics, such as shiso leaves, yuzu rind, or black peppercorns (optional)

If the ginger skin is pale cream, smooth, and nearly translucent, there is no need to peel it. If the skin is tan and a bit wrinkly, peel it off. Thinly slice the ginger crosswise with a mandoline or sharp knife. Transfer the ginger to a saucepan.

Add the vinegar, water, honey, salt, and aromatics (if using) to the pan, place over medium heat, and heat, stirring, until the honey and salt dissolve. Remove from the heat and let cool to room temperature.

Transfer the ginger and liquid to an airtight container and refrigerate for a few days before enjoying. The pickle will keep for up to 3 months.

—

Dill Pickle Spears
Makes 2–3 quarts

18–24 cucumbers, each about 5 inches long (about 8 lb)
2 handfuls of flowering dill heads
2 fresh green chiles (optional)
2–4 bay leaves
4–6 cloves garlic
2 tablespoons black peppercorns
1 teaspoon coriander seeds
1½ cups white wine vinegar
1½ cups water
¼ cup kosher salt
Pinch of sugar (optional)

Clean the cucumbers well, removing any blossom remnants on the ends. Cut them lengthwise into quarters and then pack the spears into sterilized jars or other storage containers. Divide the dill heads, chiles (if using), bay leaves, garlic, peppercorns, and coriander seeds evenly among the jars.

In a saucepan, combine the vinegar, water, salt, and sugar (if using) over medium-high heat and bring to a boil, stirring to dissolve the salt. Remove from the heat and pour the hot liquid over the cucumbers and seasonings, immersing them. Cover tightly, let cool to room temperature, and then refrigerate for a few days before enjoying. The pickles will keep for up to 3 months.

Farm Giardiniera
Makes about 4 quarts

4 quarts bite-size trimmed vegetables, such as carrots, celery, onion, peppers, and cauliflower
1 cup kosher salt
1 head garlic, cloves separated and peeled
Aromatics, such as celery seeds, fennel seeds, peppercorns, fresh oregano, or bay leaf
2 cups distilled white vinegar, plus more as needed
1 cup olive oil
1 cup neutral oil, such as grapeseed

Place the vegetables in a bowl and toss with the salt. Pour water over them to submerge fully, cover with a kitchen towel or plastic wrap, and let sit overnight on the counter. The next day, drain and rinse the vegetables. Evenly distribute them into sterilized containers and tuck in the garlic and aromatics.

In a jar, shake the vinegar with the oils and pour the mixture over the vegetables until they are fully submerged. If pieces are still poking out, top off with more vinegar. Cap the jars and let sit for a few days in the refrigerator before serving. (If you are into canning, go ahead and process the jars in a hot water bath.) The pieces can be leftwhole and eaten as a snack or blitzed up in a food processor to a relish consistency. It is phenomenal on a sandwich with aioli!

—

Carrot Jam
Makes about 2 quarts

2 lb carrots, shredded on a box grater or in a food processor fitted with the grater attachment
3 cups sugar
Grated zest and juice of 3–4 lemons
Grated zest and juice of 1–2 oranges
1–2 teaspoons kosher salt
1 tablespoon liqueur of choice or brandy (optional)
Any combination of aromatics, such as cinnamon stick, whole cloves, allspice, star anise, black peppercorns, caraway seeds, or anything else you might fancy
A few grates from a nutmeg

In a heavy-bottomed pot, combine the carrots, sugar, lemon and orange zest and juice, salt, and liqueur (if using) and mix well. Let sit for 1 hour or so to allow the sugar and salt to penetrate the carrots.

Make a sachet of your desired aromatic blend with a piece of cheesecloth and twine. Tuck the sachet into the carrots and add a bit of water along with the nutmeg. Place over medium heat and cook, stirring every so often, until the carrots take on a sheen and the liquid has thickened to a syrup consistency, 20–30 minutes. Let cool to room temperature, discard the sachet, and store in an airtight container in the refrigerator for up to a few weeks.

Note: If canning is your thing, this jam preserves beautifully. And if you want a stronger aromatic flavor, leave the sachet in the mixture overnight before discarding it.

—

Habanada Jam
Makes 2 pints

2 lb Habanada peppers, stemmed
2¼ cups sugar
2 teaspoons kosher salt
½ cup distilled white vinegar
8–12 cloves garlic, or 4-inch piece fresh ginger, peeled (optional)

Put the peppers into a food processor and blitz to a fine mash. Transfer to a shallow, wide, heavy pot and add the sugar, salt, and vinegar. If using the garlic or ginger, use a Microplane or other fine-rasp grater to grate it directly into the pot.

Place the pot over medium-low heat and cook, stirring occasionally, until the mixture has thickened, about 40 minutes. It should have a thin, gel-like texture. Remove from the heat and let cool at room temperature overnight. It will continue to thicken as it cools.

The next morning, taste the cold jam and adjust the salt or vinegar if needed. Transfer to jars, cap tightly, and store in the refrigerator for up to 2 months.

Note: For longer storage, adjust the salt and vinegar when the jam is removed from the heat and then ladle the hot jam into hot sterilized canning jars, leaving ½-inch headspace. Wipe the rims clean, cap tightly, and process in a hot water bath for 10 minutes. Store in a cool cupboard for up to 1 year.

Tomato Jam

Makes about 1 pint

About 3 cups water

6¾ cups sugar

2 pinches of kosher salt

3 lb very sweet tomatoes, peeled and chopped

1 vanilla bean

½ lemon (optional)

In a large, very thick-bottomed pot, combine the water, sugar, and salt over medium heat and bring to a boil, stirring to dissolve the sugar. Boil until a syrup forms, about 5 minutes.

Add the tomatoes, adjust the heat to maintain a gentle simmer, and simmer, stirring often to prevent scorching, for about 40 minutes. Pop in the vanilla bean and cook, continuing to stir, until the mixture is thick and sticky, 15–20 minutes.

Remove the vanilla bean, taste the jam, and adjust with salt and with a drop or two of lemon juice or a few grates of zest if needed. Skim off any scuzzy debris that has collected on the surface of the jam and then cook for a few more moments before ladling into glass jars. Cap tightly, let cool, and store in the refrigerator. It will keep for up to 2 weeks.

COMPOUND BUTTERS

Compound butters are a secret weapon of the culinary world. Rich, divinely decadent butter mixed with bold ingredients provides an easy way to infuse a simply prepared meat, fish, or vegetable with complex flavor. They can be both a schmear and a sauce and will lift whatever they top to a new level. Leftover compound butter, well wrapped, will keep for 2 weeks in the refrigerator or for 3 months in the freezer. Each recipe makes about 1 pound of compound butter.

—

Pink Peppercorn, Parmesan & Lemon Butter

1 lb soft unsalted butter

⅓ cup pink peppercorns, smashed

Grated zest of 2–3 lemons (Meyer lemons work great)

1 small shallot, minced

1 cup grated Parmesan cheese

2 teaspoons Maldon salt

Using a stand mixer with the paddle attachment or a bowl with a spatula, mix together all the ingredients until airy and combined.

Spoon the butter onto a large sheet of parchment paper or plastic wrap, roll into a log, twist the ends to seal, and refrigerate or freeze until ready to use.

—

Spicy Orange Honey Butter

1 lb soft unsalted soft butter

⅔ cup runny honey

2–3 teaspoons Maldon salt

2–3 teaspoons hot chile powder, such as cayenne

Grated zest of 1 orange

Using a stand mixer with the paddle attachment or a bowl with a spatula, mix together all the ingredients until airy and combined.

Spoon the butter onto a large sheet of parchment paper or plastic wrap, roll into a log, twist the ends to seal, and refrigerate or freeze until ready to use.

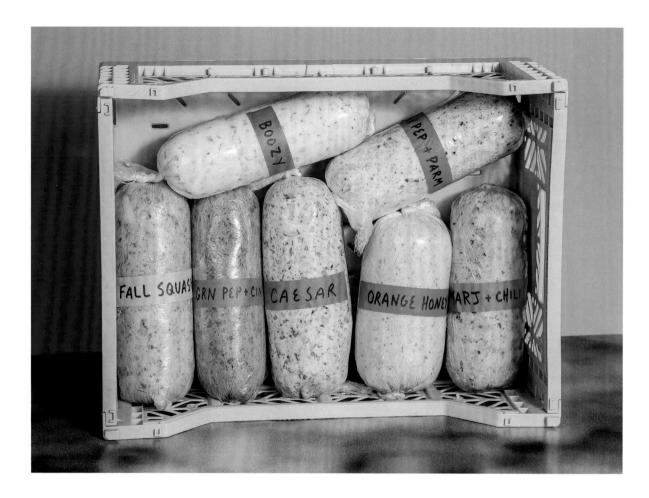

Caesar Butter

1 lb soft unsalted butter

4–6 anchovy fillets in olive oil, finely chopped

1 shallot, minced

½ cup capers, rinsed and roughly chopped

½ cup chopped soft fresh herbs, such as flat-leaf parsley, dill, or basil

Grated zest of 2 lemons

Pinch of red chile flakes

Kosher salt

Using a stand mixer with the paddle attachment or a bowl with a spatula, mix together all the ingredients except the salt until airy and combined. The anchovies and capers both have salt that will perfume the butter, but give it a taste to see if you want more.

Spoon the butter onto a large sheet of parchment paper or plastic wrap, roll into a log, twist the ends to seal, and refrigerate or freeze until ready to use.

Chile & Fresh Marjoram Butter

3–4 cloves garlic, chopped

2 tablespoons olive oil

Handful of fresh hot chiles or ⅓ cup Calabrian chiles in oil, finely chopped

1 lb soft unsalted butter

⅓ cup chopped fresh marjoram or oregano

Grated zest of 1 lemon

2 teaspoons Maldon salt

In a skillet, sauté the garlic and fresh chiles in the oil over medium-low heat until soft. If using chiles in oil, skip sautéing them. Let cool.

Using a stand mixer with the paddle attachment or a bowl with a spatula, mix together all the ingredients until airy and combined.

Spoon the butter onto a large sheet of parchment paper or plastic wrap, roll into a log, twist the ends to seal, and refrigerate or freeze until ready to use.

Garlic Scape Butter

1 cup finely chopped garlic scapes
Olive oil, for sautéing if needed
1 lb soft unsalted butter
3–4 teaspoons Maldon salt
Big pinch of grated lemon zest

If the garlic scapes are very fibrous, give them a quick sauté in a bit of olive oil until soft. If the scapes are young and tender to the tooth, they will be just fine raw.

Using a stand mixer with the paddle attachment or a bowl with a spatula, mix together all the ingredients until airy and combined.

Spoon the butter onto a large sheet of parchment paper or plastic wrap, roll into a log, twist the ends to seal, and refrigerate or freeze until ready to use.

Note: This is equally good with ramp tops, should you be lucky enough to find them. Sauté just until soft, then combine with the butter.

—

Boozy Butter

1 lb soft unsalted butter
Big splash of booze of choice, such as whiskey, vermouth, sherry, port, Pernod, or Grand Marnier
¼ cup minced shallot and/or 3–4 cloves garlic, minced (optional)
2–3 teaspoons Maldon salt
Bit of finely chopped fresh flat-leaf parsley
Pinch of grated lemon zest

Using a stand mixer with the paddle attachment or a bowl with a spatula, mix together all of the ingredients until airy and combined.

Spoon the butter onto a large sheet of parchment paper or plastic wrap, roll into a log, twist the ends to seal, and refrigerate or freeze until ready to use.

Note: You can add an additional herb depending on your liquor choice. A woody herb, such as thyme or rosemary, works well with darker spirits, such as whiskey, while tarragon and chervil are good with lighter ones, such as vermouth or Pernod.

Fall Squash & Maple Butter

1–1½ lb fall squash of choice, peeled, seeded, and cubed
2 splashes of aged sherry vinegar
Olive oil, for drizzling
Kosher salt
1 lb soft unsalted butter
½ cup finely chopped fresh sage or marjoram leaves
¼ cup pure dark maple syrup
2–4 teaspoons Maldon salt
Many large cracks fresh black pepper

Preheat the oven to 400°F. Pile the squash on a sheet pan and toss with a splash of the vinegar, a drizzle of oil, and a big pinch of salt. Spread in a single layer and bake until soft, about 20 minutes. Let cool, then mash by hand or whirl in a food processor until smooth. Measure ⅔ cup for the butter. Reserve the remainder for another use.

Using a stand mixer with the paddle attachment or a bowl with a spatula, mix together all the ingredients until airy and combined.

Spoon the butter onto a large sheet of parchment paper or plastic wrap, roll into a log, twist the ends to seal, and refrigerate or freeze until ready to use.

—

Green Peppercorn, Garlic & Cinnamon Butter

2–4 cloves garlic, finely chopped
2 tablespoons olive oil
1 lb soft unsalted butter
¼ cup drained green peppercorns, crushed
1–2 teaspoons ground cinnamon
2 teaspoons Maldon salt
Few big cracks fresh black pepper
Bit of chopped fresh flat-leaf parsley, for color (optional)

In a small skillet, sauté the garlic in the oil over medium-low heat until soft. Let cool.

Using a stand mixer with the paddle attachment or a bowl with a spatula, mix together all the ingredients until airy and combined.

Spoon the butter onto a large sheet of parchment paper or plastic wrap, roll into a log, twist the ends to seal, and refrigerate or freeze until ready to use.

INDEX

Note: Page references in *italics* indicate photographs.

ACKNOWLEDGMENTS

With much love and gratitude . . .

Firstly, thank you to all of the people who work so hard to make Forts Ferry Farm happen every day behind the scenes without even asking for an ounce of credit. You know who you are.

Creating, writing, styling, and photographing this book entirely by ourselves was an amazing adventure and learning experience. Thank you to my business partners, John Barker and James Barker.

John, thank you for your unwavering support and patience. You have been my sounding board throughout this entire process, and I couldn't ask for a better father for our son or best friend. I love you.

James, I am so grateful for your keen eye. These pages wouldn't not be what they are without your photography. You're my forever cookbook photo companion and I love creating with you.

Matt and Shannon, thank you for believing in me, always having my back, and testing these recipes to make sure they were the best they could possibly be. I am indebted to you both.

To our farm team—Ivana, Sarah, and Julia—you make hard work look easy. Thank you for growing the beautiful and delicious things that have inspired these pages. Your hard work does not go unnoticed.

Anchalee, you have been by my side, with all of my brands, for nearly two decades now. Thank you for your talents and opinions, and for always pushing our vibe to premium heights.

My publishers, Amy Marr and Roger Shaw, book designer Debbie Berne, and all the wonderful people at Weldon Owen and Insight Editions. Thank you for taking another chance on me with this second book and cheers to many more chances to come! It has been a blast bringing this book to life with you all.

My parents, who have been by my side always, in every moment, good or bad. Thank you for being my best friends and the best parents I could ever ask for. You have given me all that I have needed, and so much more.

My son, George, you are my greatest teacher and the coolest person I have ever met or made. Thank you for choosing me to be your mom. It's the greatest gift I could have ever asked for.

Lastly, thank you to all of those people who have come and gone in my life and doubted my abilities. Your doubts have only expanded my capacities, and I truly know that absolutely anything is possible.

From the bottom of my heart, thank you to all.

"This is my invariable advice to people: Learn how to cook—try new recipes, learn from your mistakes, be fearless, and above all have fun."
—Julia Childs

weldon**owen**

an imprint of Insight Editions
PO Box 3088
San Rafael, CA 94912
www.weldonowen.com

Library of Congress Cataloging-in-
Publication data is available.

ISBN-13: 979-8-88674-082-0

The information in this book is provided as
a resource for inspiration and education.
Author and Publisher expressly disclaim
any responsibility for any adverse
effects from the use or application of
the information contained in this book.
Neither the Publisher nor Author shall be
liable for any losses suffered by any reader
of this book.

Weldon Owen would also like to thank
Rachel Markowitz, Elizabeth Parson, and
Sharon Silva.

CEO: Raoul Goff
VP Publisher: Roger Shaw
Associate Publisher: Amy Marr
Publishing Director: Katie Killebrew
VP Creative: Chrissy Kwasnik
VP Manufacturing: Alix Nicholaeff
Sr Production Manager: Joshua Smith
Sr Production Manager, Subsidiary Rights:
    Lina s Palma-Temena

Photographer: James Barker
Designer: Debbie Berne

Insight Editions, in association with Roots of
Peace, will plant two trees for each tree used
in the manufacturing of this book. Roots
of Peace is an internationally renowned
humanitarian organization dedicated to
eradicating land mines worldwide and
converting war-torn lands into productive
farms and wildlife habitats. Roots of Peace
will plant two million fruit and nut trees in
Afghanistan and provide farmers there
with the skills and support necessary for
sustainable land use.